MASSIMILIANO SERPE

DON'T FORGET TO TAKE OUT THE GARLIC

TALES AND RECIPES FROM THE NEAPOLITAN WONDERLAND

100 RECIPES FROM DAILY NEAPOLITAN CUISINE, SIMPLY EXPLAINED, WITH LITTLE NUGGETS OF HISTORY AND LEGEND, A SAUCERFUL OF SECRETS, FUN FACTS, HELPFUL TIPS, AND BURNING, SIZZLING PASSION

Titolo | Don't forget to take out the garlic
Autore | Massimiliano Serpe
ISBN | 978-88-31671-95-8

Youcanprint
Via Marco Biagi 6, 73100 Lecce
www.youcanprint.it
info@youcanprint.it

To my mother,
for teaching me the joy of living.
To my wife, Lucia,
for holding me tight even when I wasn't there.
To my sons, Davide and Giuseppe,
so that they may one day grow into fine men.

Written by
Massimiliano Serpe
With the Support of
Lucia Loffredo, Giuseppe and Davide Serpe
Photography
Massimiliano Serpe
Artwork
Laura Bonito
Graphic Design
Massimiliano Serpe
Typesetting
Alberto Laterza
English Translation
F. Balzano

Summary

Pasta Dishes

Minestra and Soups

Main Course

Desserts

Sweets, Pastries, Salty and Sweet Cookies

Liquors

Conserves

The Italian version of this book, released in November 2019, was titled "A Napoli anche l'Aglio è nato con la Camicia": that is, unfortunately, scarcely translatable wordplay describing someone's privileged social status, in this case applied to garlic as an essential and irreplaceable ingredient in Neapolitan cuisine.

As you will find out in the following introduction, the idea of writing a book sprung into my mind after spending some time abroad, where, working in the restaurant business, I had the chance to meet a lot of people, among them many fellow Italians who always loved to stay and chew the fat… along with some fine traditional food, too. The world is rife with Italian restaurants full to bursting with clients that want to get to know and taste our food. Tourists come in droves to our peninsula all year long, not only to see the sights, but for some good eating, too. Our compatriots living abroad have long since changed their culinary habits, but I found out that virtually all of them wish to return to the traditions of their homeland, even if it's simply by reading a book.

And I, too, had my wish granted: my book will reach an even wider, international audience, thanks to the work of my nephew, Fabio, who dedicated himself to translating it and making it an even more pleasant, useful and interesting experience.

Introduction

I'll be the first to admit that I don't read as much as I should, aside from cookbooks and the occasional work-related document, but I consider it a rare gift to be properly book-smart and learn quickly from what you read.

The first thing I thought about, when I had the idea of writing a cookbook, is that millions suffer the pangs of hunger each day, while in the western world food is more than plenty. For every child that would treat a bowl of fried rice as manna from heaven, there's another that throws away his snack because he doesn't quite like the dark chocolate glaze. Being self-aware of our own consumerism becomes, then, a necessity. In the following pages I offer you my reflections, born within and without the Self, on an issue that we should take more seriously both individually and as a community.

Since I was only a little boy, I was fascinated by everything going on in the kitchen, from the necessary shopping for ingredients to the table's setup. I spent many mornings in the market, mesmerized by the swirling colors and lights, the fragrant smells and the figures always coming and going, so busy living in those narrow alleyways where the practice of the merchant craft paved the way for genuine human bonds.

I'd never have guessed that this passion of mine would allow me, one day, to work in this field. Granted, I am a stranger in a strange land, but without those wonderful experiences, this book wouldn't even exist.

I wrote it together with my wife Lucia, also a cooking aficionado, and with more than a little help from my sons Davide and Giuseppe, who are all too ready to judge my cooking, challenge me in my tastes, and more.

Food, like almost everything that's even remotely linked to an economic interest, has gone global; as a result, many dishes lost their characteristic, old-time taste, and it's hard to find something truly "authentic". Those who belong to our generation are already used from a young age to eating low-quality, mass-produced canned food that tastes like salted concrete. Nobody really knows the genuine taste and textures of old, and how could they? Everything that's made that is good enough to set a trend is instantly mass-produced to oblivion, saturating the market and inevitably watering down its taste.

My job as an entrepreneur and then as an aspiring chef allowed me to travel all around Europe and savor all kinds of different foods. I had the distinct impression that we're all being manipulated into consuming what is labeled as "genuine", but is really of questionable quality and even more questionable origin.

In Italy, we take cooking seriously and we're rightly recognized for it on the global market, but the same process of manipulation and mass production in our country has reached heights that border on outrage.

The aftertaste of certain dishes lingers in our mind, inexorably linked to a particular experience, or even to someone we once loved, or still love. When I was only a boy, people felt strongly about our tradition of home-cooking, more than today. Simple, everyday ingredients were the foundation of every good meal; on Sundays or during the holidays, with the whole family gathered around the kitchen table, dishes became a little more complex, with varied ingredients and different processes. Many recipes are directly derived from those very same Sunday gatherings, maybe only slightly more… generous than they were back then.

I still have a vivid memory of all the different aromas swirling in the central alleyways on a Sunday morning, a colour that changed according to the time of day: from the sweet-sour smell of *salsa al ragù* for the *soffritto,* to the fried vegetables that intoned the prelude to a *parmigiana,* and all the way to a traditional fried-fish *paranza* or the smoky aftertaste of grilled meat.

Back in the day, when you could, lunch or dinner were spent together with someone familiar, and chances were high they'd prepare that pasta dish, or that sweet dessert, that you liked so much; back then, you could ask your grandma to cook you that one "thing" that your mother just had no time to prepare anymore. But time you had, and you could spend all day at your nana's home watching in awe as she lovingly prepared everything that was needed, all the ingredients, pots and pans, to make a wonderful treat taste truly "authentic".

And what about the tradition of preserves, often prepared during specific times of the year, because only in those small frames the fruits of the earth were ripe enough to be worked on: tomatoes, eggplant, artichokes, peppers were a mainstay in a housewife's kitchen, and each had a different way of keeping them from spoiling; you could store them doused in oil or vinegar, or with a sweet-sour mix, according to the needs of each type of vegetable. Tomato preserves were especially favoured, and each family actually had its own particular way of preparing them, its own little tips and tricks to make them taste better.

Another common sight in those times was homemade liquor: in nearly every house in Torre del Greco you could have a glass of *Limoncello* or *Nocillo* in good company, its recipe usually passed down through the generations and prepared rigorously "by heart" or with tools that were far removed from our modern scales. Often these adventures in distillation were a good reason to let the neighbors gather round, share their ingredients and eventually partake of the distilled liquor.

These are only a few of the stories that have by now faded from this world, and that let us grow into healthy adults.

Massimiliano Serpe

Foreword

If we were to take Feuerbach at his word, then we could freely state that "you are what you eat". I beg the German master forgiveness then, and humbly loan his aphorism (that he certainly didn't mean to use in the foreword of a cookbook) for my analysis on the reason why the culinary habits of a man shape his sensibilities.

Before we start, we have to admit that the sensibilities of someone born in the south of Italy, especially for us "country folk", are as unknowable as the wind, obscure but brilliant at the same time, nostalgic yet prescient, solitary yet welcoming. He who cooks stumbles in the dark, dazed and confused, devoid of clear ideas, until the advice of a loved one lights the path to resolution. Even the rejection of such advice or observation can open a doorway to clarity, morph doubt into certainty, hesitation in decisive action. He who cooks, does so for his children, to whom he shows the value of history.

He does so for his mother and father, to whom he reminds of the primal and bittersweet feeling of nostalgia, working together with memory, like Proust himself remembered and wrote about *la Petite Madeleine*: that small, delicious treat whose taste brought him back to his childhood home, to his mother's routine, to the smells that lingered in the kitchen, the voices that sifted through the air, the cold cutting through his windows in the morning causing the author to curl up shivering.

Sons and daughters discover, parents mull over, meditate.

He who cooks, does so after work (for if you cook, time has to be on your side, as it triggers the red flame of emotion, and having little or none of it means neither inspiration nor rapture will overtake you), when he's alone: the perfect time to be in touch with one's inner taste, but at the same time being aware that each person and occasion is a world unto itself, and when cooking, he should not follow his selfish desire to offer the same trite dishes he likes making. "Do you like chives?", "Do you mind if I add just a little bit of pepper?".

Communication: the starting point to learn about the Other, to socialize, to accept, especially when the Other is ready to die on the hill of his convictions, maybe with candor and even rudeness; as when the Other opposes resistance, the Self hardens, impregnable (and homes are always heavy with old wounds, unspoken arguments and all-too-spoken little zings that come expectedly or not).

There are but some of the emotional dynamics that occur when someone cooks or eats well, in the south and beyond. This is valid (of course) for those who have a keen sense of taste that is not only biological, but full of awareness.

And are you, dear Reader, merely biological or fully aware?

The discourse about cuisine was certainly spearheaded by the authors of the past. Writers, philosophers, playwrights, men of learning who, tackling a plethora different topics in their works, all too often skirted in the realm of cooking. Some of them employ the culinary arts as a background or as a literary device to engineer plot twists or introduce new developments in their stories, like the aforementioned Marcel Proust. Another artist I would like to (rightfully) mention, in this regard, is our very own actor and playwright Eduardo de Filippo. In addition to the numerous culinary references in his body of work (above all, in his plays), Eduardo began writing about cooking in the 60s.

It's a little known fact, and even less known, I understand, for a foreign audience. De Filippo, for us, represents the reality of what it means to be Neapolitan. His wife, Isabella Quarantotti, decided in 2001 to publish a small booklet, "Si cucine commevogl'i" ("If I cook the way I like it"), in which we can find numerous recipes which were quite dear to Eduardo, and ones which he wanted to honor. The ones that were the most delicious, the ones that sparked memories of the past, were they pleasant or unpleasant, the ones who mattered the most.

It's to be understood that cooking, an activity which most would find trivial, is truly anything but. "A simple, ordinary occurrence in our lives", or so they say. Yet, this ordinary occurrence becomes extraordinary in the imagination of the attuned, becoming a story of romance, and therefore a fantastic creation.

A lesser known author in this field is Manuel Vàzquez Montalbàn, Spanish essayist and journalist, who wrote a satirical cookbook in 1992 called "The Immoral Recipes". The work had the same premises as my father's own cookbook, more or less: no great ambitions, with a kindred spirit of sharing and the necessary wit to lighten the mood.

Moving forward, we can find the book "L'Assaggiatrice" by Giuseppina Torregrossa, a story about taste and sexuality, and stumble upon the "magical chef" archetype in Joanne Harris' "Chocolat", in which the *patissier* is able to cure her clients of any illnesses with a simple application of *ad-hoc* pastries. As we can see, when we write or inquire about cooking, we have to consider that it is a common experience in everyone's life, from the writer to the musician, from the electrician to the valet, from the chef to the policeman; and thus, if we want to truly talk about cooking, we must be aware of what truly sets it apart from everything else: universality.

Davide Serpe

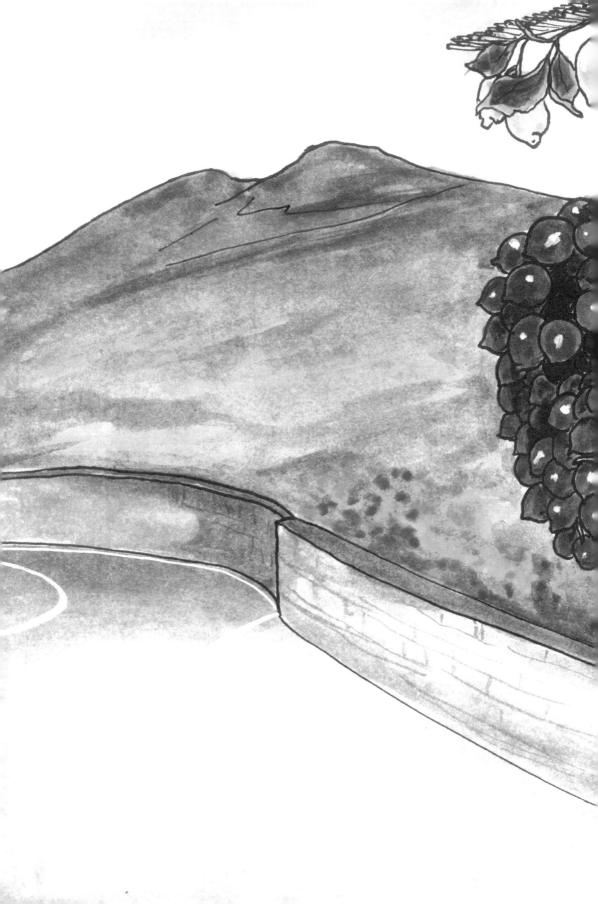

The Ingredients

The peculiar location of Campania, surrounded by both fertile soil and seawater, allowed for a plethora of prime raw material to be derived both from agriculture and fishing, giving our cooking a selection of dishes that is centuries old.

In those times, the modern, transformative techniques that allowed food to be preserved for ages simply didn't exist: people had to grow accustomed to what the earth had to offer season by season.

Each one of us should strive to apply one simple idea, even though it may not be easy due to time constraints or some confusion derived from media overload: we have to cook with humble ingredients, local ingredients, paying respect to seasonality; that will allow us to make healthy, tasty food in a time and money-efficient way.

It's quite easy to weigh the price of an out-of-season (around march), mostly tasteless bell pepper against our actual need for one, and just avoid buying altogether.

Before delving into the many delicacies that made our region's cooking world-renowned, I would like to introduce (if nothing else, to honor the title of this book) the one ingredient that truly made each of our recipes special, to the point of being essential to the taste of many of our foods: garlic, or in our tongue, *aglio*.

Peeled or unpeeled, raw or cooked, every which way it's used, garlic holds a special spot in our hearts. It is found and cultivated in Campania near the town of Ufita, near Avellino, and it is considered of excellent quality: its cloves are medium-sized and usually of a white-pinkish color, and it takes its name from the town it comes from (*aglio d'Ufita*). Excellence also comes in the form of its "big sister", the onion, which is found in the towns of Montoro and Alife, both variants known and appreciated in Campania and beyond.

In the following paragraphs, I will continue to explore and describe these outstanding goods that made, and still make, our cuisine unique.

Il pane ∾ *Bread*

The region of Campania is rife with different customary bread-making techniques and little rituals, most of them belonging to different areas within the region itself: the *pane Cafone,* sold in large round chunks the color of hay, thick and crusty, typically found in the Camaldoli near Naples, but prevalent in many areas of the northern hinterland; the town of Villaricca boasts an impressive bread-making tradition that dates back centuries, to the point that its name used to be *Panicocoli* (a term, *Panicuocole,* that came from our dialect and whose roots can be found in the Latin language, roughly meaning "to cook bread"). Its products are sought after in the whole country, and usually sold in round *panielli* or slender *panelle*.

The bakers of San Sebastiano al Vesuvio are equally as famous. They are masters of the acclaimed *Palatone,* a long loaf of delicious white bread with a thin crust that stays fresh for days.

The bread from Montecalvo, tall with a thick crust and a little cavity on the inside to signify its quality, is instead quite known and appreciated near Avellino. In the same area, which is called *Alta Irpinia,* another kind of special, very ancient bread is produced, the *Calitri. I*t is typically round in shape and vertically cut, but its uniqueness comes mainly from its weight: the round shapes, called "*ruote e' carrett*" (lit. wheelbarrow wheels), can reach a whopping 6 kilos.

The plateaus of Irpinia also offer its farmers a particular kind of Rye, which is called *grano di Iermano* or *Ciurmano* in local dialect. It is usually mixed with durum wheat to make up the essential ingredient of a very old bread recipe, the *pane di Iurmano,* dark in color and of long-lasting freshness.

Moving to the Sannio area around Benevento, we can instead find a special kind of Rye bread made from an old breed of durum wheat, called *saragolla,* which also gives the bread its name; its taste is robust, its crust thick and its colour is a faded yellow.

In Padula, near Salerno, one can instead find a delightful, homemade loaf called *pane di Padula,* which comes in round shapes of about two kilos each, squared on the top like the *panis quadratus* depicted in the roman murals in Pompeii. Its taste and freshness can be preserved for up to 15 days.

The so-called *pan biscotto* (*biscuit bread*) comes instead from Agerola, and presents a pleasurable rustic taste that meshes wonderfully with the local dishes and goods. The singular virtue of this type of bread, resulting from both its ingredients and its handicraft, is that it is possible to dip it in water before consuming it, giving it the fresh, spongy taste it's known for.

I latticini ⁊ Dairy

What we call today *mozzarella di bufala* (buffalo mozzarella) appeared as a term for the first time in a 1570 manuscript by Italian chef and author Bartolomeo Scappi, even though the term *mozza* (which means *cut* or *chopped*) seemed to be already in use before that. The origin of this Mediterranean delicacy seems to predate even the first millennium, though, since the buffalo was imported in Italy by the Lombards in the 6th Century. The manufacture of dairy products in Campania goes way beyond *mozzarella,* even though it remains its most appreciated and known product worldwide. There are many other local treats that make us proud in the food market, like the *ricotta di fuscella,* special light ricotta that's sold in little baskets, usually eaten fresh as a single dish and rarely used in the kitchen, its light and delicate taste making it an excellent choice of appetizer. In the city markets of my youth, it came wrapped inside a vine leaf.

The *bocconcini del Cardinale* are equally as delicious, consisting of little bites of mozzarella that aren't brined, instead being dipped directly in cream or milk. They're usually sold in *langelle*, which are simple terracotta vases.

Often used in cooking, *provola affumicata* (smoked *provola*) is a kind of mozzarella exposed to woodsmoke after packaging; as a result, it turns dark brown on the outside, while the inside keeps the usual white-ivory colour, gaining a very distinctive taste. The *fior di latte* goes through a similar process, but the final outcome is different in both colour and texture. *Scamorza* is also made in quite the same way, save for a little adjustment that makes it develop a thick outer shell. It is often smoked, and it comes in round or caciocavallo shapes.

The *provolone* family, rich in taste and variations, goes from its "youngest" member, the tiny and sugary-sweet *provoloncino bebé,* to the medium sized sweet or spicy provolone. A well-known variant is the *provolone del monaco*, produced on the Lattari Mountains. Another great-quality product is the *caciocavallo,* an offshoot of provolone that mainly differs in its texture and the classic "flagon" shape with the equally customary choke on top that ends in the *capa,* or head, of the *caciocavallo.* Finely-aged *caciocavallo* is usually grated.

The areas of production are usually the ones traditionally used for pasture, like the Cilento, Aversa or Agerola, whose plains are most suited to this kind of activity.

Pasta

The tradition of handmade pasta runs even stronger in the small municipalities of the hinterland. In the province of Avellino and Benevento, *fusilli, cavatelli* and *maccheroni* are still made with rudimentary tools, while strictly "Neapolitan" cuisine prefers the industrially-produced durum wheat flour pasta.

Large scale pasta production in the area dates back at the very least to the XVI century, when the ideal conditions to dry and preserve pasta were discovered in the city of Gragnano. Local variations on the classic shapes live alongside their more famous ancestors, like for examples *paccheri* and *ziti,* which are snapped in twain by hand before cooking and seasoning. *Pasta ammescata* (mixed pasta) is usually made out of the broken leftovers of this process, and used to be sold at a smaller price because of it. It pairs exceptionally well with legumes of all kinds, from lentils to beans.

Two other great contenders are *gnocchi* (which, I found out, are especially hard to pronounce right for a foreign crowd who has no concept of a soft *gn* sound), made of a mixture of flour and mashed potatoes, and *scialatielli,* currently trending with all kinds of seafood recipes.

Verdure e Ortaggi ✷ *Vegetables*

The quintessential Neapolitan veggie is undoubtedly the *friariello,* a kind of bitter-ish escarole, along with many varieties of broccoli, savoy, *minestra* mixes and *puntarelle* (a type of asparagus). Zucchini are widely used, too, and the biggest ones are cooked *alla scapece,* basically bathed *(scapece* is derived from Spanish *escabeche,* which means "to dip"), while still hot, in a mixture of oil, vinegar, parsley and garlic. Smaller ones are usually fried and seasoned with salt, vinegar and fresh mint. Additionally, the zucchini flowers can be caked in batter and deep-fried.

The *zucchetta di pergola* or *zucchetta del prete* is a small pumpkin with a delicate, sweet aftertaste, often paired with pasta or a tomato soup.

Peppers come in all shapes and sizes, from the medium-sized ones (either red or yellow) to the less imposing, sweet green peppers, which are often fried.

The name *mammarella* denotes a particularly valued type of artichoke, relatively massive in size, round-shaped with purple-hued leaves.

Salads are the side dish of choice for many meals, especially those revolving around seafood. Many choose the crispier *incappucciata* over the common lettuce, and regularly mix it with fennel, rocket (that used to be sold by street vendors along with the less refined *pucchiacchella)* and radish (if you want to stick to tradition, then get the longer, spicier ones instead of the round, sweet ones; they've become really hard to find lately, though).

Tomatoes were first imported back in the 16th century by Spanish wayfarers from the Americas, though nobody really cared about them for more than two centuries. It was only in the turn of the 19th century when people began squeezing tomato sauce in every other recipe, and the higher demand led to an increase in the farming of tomatoes in Campania, to the point of it becoming one of its lead produce. One of the finer varieties in Campania is the *San Marzano,* along with the so-called *grape tomato* or *pomodorino 'do piennolo.* Tomato salads are a veritable lifesaver in the excruciatingly hot Italian summer, and are typically seasoned with onions, oregano and/or basil, and olive oil.

Legumes are a mainstay in every kitchen, from beans (which come in vastly different varieties, like *Controne, Casalbuono Occhio Nero di Oliveto Citra, Regina di Gorga, "a paisiello" or Mandia)* to the lentils of Colliano, once again to the small, round, golden chickpeas of Cicerale (which are incredibly difficult to farm) and all the way to the *Maracuoccio of Lentiscosa* (which belongs to the *cicerchia* family), the *dead man's tooth* from Acerra and the *giant lupine* from Vairano.

La frutta ∾ *Fruits*

Thanks to the tireless effort and rustic wisdom of our farmers, the fruits of the Campanian soil are known and appreciated all over the world, often earning multiple medals and quality stamps from the international community. Many of these products figure in a lot of dinner tables, both home and abroad.

The oldest fruit in all the land is actually the *Mela Annurca*, a unique bright red apple. Its colour is the result of a particular "reddening" process that takes place in specially-made, overshadowed apple gardens, where the ambient light lets the fruit ripe to its characteristic full red.

It's by no means an easy feat, especially since the apples have to be turned periodically on their bed of pine needles or wooden splints, to ensure they are fully exposed to the light. The fruit itself is rich in fibers, improves intestinal function and is a good diuretic, recommended both for children and the elderly; not to mention, it is often included in diets for the sickly and particularly diabetes sufferers. An apple a day keeps the doctor away, quite literally!

Lemons are used in a plethora of local recipes, from appetizers to desserts. The *babbà al limoncello,* spongy sweets soaked in a lemon-based liquor, are extremely well-liked, as are *delizie* and lemon sorbet. Recently it's been hypothesized that the Lama gurus, nestled in the heights of the Himalayas, had been the first one to discover the medicinal properties of Lemon, even though we owe the Arabian peoples for the first attempts at farming the fruit.

The farming techniques haven't changed all that much since then. The lemon plants are held up by chestnut wood scaffolding, and each season they're placed under special coverings that both protect the fruit from the elements and slow down their growth.

The Montella chestnut is considered one of the best in the entire country, and it was the only fruit and vegetable product to be granted the prestigious DOC (protected designation of origin) qualification by the Italian Ministry of Agriculture (it would nine years later be replaced by the similar IGP). It's farmed in the municipalities of Montella, Bagnoli Irpino, Cassano Irpino, Nusco, Volturara Irpina and Montemarano. The distinctive features of this fine chestnut are its full texture, light saltiness and exceptional preservability. Perfect for meat seasoning or soups, it's best used as a base or supplement for pastries and cakes. It's also often baked in the oven and eaten as a treat in Christmas time.

One of the finest Italian hazelnuts comes from Giffoni, and it's called *Tonda di Giffoni.* It was already common in the 11th century around the Imo Valley and the Picentini Mountains near Salerno, and takes its name from a small hamlet in the area. Possessing a full texture and aroma, white in color and with an easily removable film, the *Tonda di Giffoni* is particularly suited to mass production due to its features, like its perfect roundness, that make it ideal to be toasted, weighed and peeled.

There are at least a dozen names for apricots in our area, Boccuccia Liscia, Boccuccia Spinosa, Pellecchiella, Ceccona, Palummella, Vitillo, San Castrese, Fracasso, Cafona, Baracca. Each variety marks a different territory belonging to one of 18 towns in the Province, all around the Vesuvius National Park. Each have traits that make them unique, like their size, the fullness of their aroma, the smoothness of their skin or their taste; and traits that make them sisters, like their sugary yellow pulp, the pungent smell, and the yellow-orange colour of their peel, usually punctuated with faded red spots.

The *Marrone di Roccadaspide* is a round-shaped, medium-sized fruit of a dark brown color with faded stripes. The seed is wrapped in light, easily peeled film and the pulp is juicy and sweet. The production area is located in the Alburni Mountains, in the valleys of the Calore River and part of the Cilento and Vallo di Diano Reserve.

The so called White Fig of Cilento is often called the "poor man's treasure", due to the fact that it is one of the only edible foods in the area that used to be easily farmed and preserved. Dried out for a whole year, the Fig of Cilento was also a sought-out delicacy for many a rich connoisseur, to the point that trade around it flourished as far back as the 15th century. Figs can be worked into many different shapes and recipes, from enjoying it raw or dried out, to mashing into jam or syrup.

Good quality walnuts are farmed all over the region, but the best *Noce di Sorrento* can only be found in the Sorrento Peninsula. They are exported and appreciated the world over, and used in the confectionery industry or other ventures, like distilleries.

The *Serino* chestnut stands out among its competition and is divided in two local varieties: *Montemarano* and *Verdole*. The first one, also called either *Santimango* or *Marrone di Avellino*, is one of the prime specimens in Italy and can be recognized by its medium-large size, milky-white seed and sweet, crunchy pulp.

Persimmon fields began sprouting all over Campania in the last century, and we soon became one of the nation's leading producers thanks to the region's fitting climate. The area dedicated to persimmon farming is still quite large and encompasses different towns, like Pozzuoli, Acerra, Maddaloni and Pagani. The singular, or maybe plural virtues of this fruit are its hefty weight and delightful taste, mostly thanks to the sheer amount of sugar siphoned from the soil during growth.

Della Recca, Malizia, Lustra, Cornaiola are some of the many varieties of *neapolitan cherry* that all share some particular features, like higher-than-average quality, medium-large size, juicy, scented pulp and propensity for transportation and transformation. Cherries are usually picked to be eaten fresh, but they can also be made into syrups, juices, sweets, jams and liquors, in addition to being a favourite among bakers.

Percoca, from Neapolitan *percuoco,* owes its fortune to the delicate taste of Neapolitans, who crowned it Queen of the summer table since the early 18th century. *Percoche drowned in wine* are a Sunday ritual in the *Mezzogiorno*, possibly introduced by our Spanish overlords in the past centuries, as it is very similar to their *sangria*.

I pesci ∽ *Fish*

No Neapolitan kitchen is truly complete without a little bit of seafood, and we aren't really so picky with what we choose: anchovies, sardines and blue fish are usually cooked fresh off the boat with quick recipes, while redfish, weevers and *cuocci* are typically stewed in soups; medium and large-sized fish, like bass, breams, snappers, sargus and *pezzogne* are reserved for special occasions. There's plenty of less imposing sea life in the seafood stalls of the city markets, like *cicinielli,* blue fish whitebait, tiny and transparent, stewed or batter fried; or *fravagli*, a few centimeters long, chiefly made out of mullet, or *retunni,* to be caked in flour and flash-fried.

Paranza is a typical dish for which we use a particular mix of easily fried, tiny-to-small fish like small cods, mullets, soles etc. Octopus, squid and calamari are also used often, in addition to crustaceans and assorted seafood like mussels, clams, razor clams, cockles, *taratufi, fasolari, sconcigli e maruzzielli*, which are all local varieties.

And lastly, codfish, imported from the Northern Sea, is a traditional ingredient, often fried or cooked along with potatoes and tomatoes.

Le carni ∽ *Meat*

Our cuisine doesn't make great use of beef, mostly because there aren't many farms in our area that breed specifically for beef production. There are exceptions, though, like the legendary *ragù,* that also makes use of pork, which is a little more widespread.

Sausages in Naples are chiefly cut in a roundabout, lazy way, that we define *a ponta e' curtiello,* or *tip o' the knife. Cervellatine* are an interesting variation, as they're cut thinner than ordinary sausage.

Entrails, bowels and all things offal are commonly found in street food stalls, along with pig liver, wrapped in a thin layer of fat and a laurel, *tripe* and the classic *o' pere e o'musso,* which, as the name states, is literally the feet and snout of a pig, traditionally served with a healthy sprinkle of fresh lemon; spicy *soffritto* soup is often used as sauce for pasta or *freselle,* a side of dried bread that comes in slices or "donuts".

Cicoli are another delicious treat derived from the fattest layers of a pig, which are pressed to squeeze out the Sugna. Sugna is simply concentrated liquid fat, and it was often used as an alternative to olive oil in the past.

Salumi ∼ *Cold Cuts*

Regarding the production of cured meat in the Campania territory, there are many valuable products being sold, but the king is undoubtedly the *salame Napoli,* whose defining characteristic is the presence of both juicy meat and large chunks of delicious fat. *Capocollo* is another typical product, mostly enjoyed around Easter time, and dried or soft cicoli, paired with bread. A sandwich with cicoli, ricotta and pepper is a typical treat.

"*The cooking of a society is a language into which it unconsciously translates its structure*"

Claude Levi Strauss

Street Food

"Guai e maccarune se servene cauri."

"Trouble and pasta are always served hot."

Neapolitan proverb

Street Food

The latest and greatest social sensation that's trending all over the world, kept under a keen judging eye from different organizations like the FAO that track its growing numbers, commonly known in Italian parlance as... street food.

The lifestyle we lead today is the main cause of this phenomenon, especially the rampant consumerism that constantly keeps us zipping from one place to another. It's only logical then, that we'd start to eat standing, or even on the move.

But I'm digressing. Even though the hustle and bustle of modern life has certainly shifted our relationship with food, *street food* in Naples is far from a recent discovery: *au contraire,* it is a tradition that dates back to the humble beginnings of Neapolitan cuisine.

The undisputed Queen of street food is Pizza, which has become an internationally-recognized symbol- when in Naples, do as the Neapolitans do, and eat it *"a portafoglio",* folded in two and wrapped fresh from the oven in a layer of straw paper, with classic tomato sauce and mozzarella or an even juicier filling of ricotta and cicoli. Countless papers have been written on the ideal pizza dough, over time refining the kneading techniques, ingredients, leavening times and cooking methods. In the name of simplicity and budgeting, I only offer a single, foolproof recipe that is sure to result in an even quality dough, judging by the above criteria.

In the south of Italy, the street food tradition is passed down through generations, and one can find all sorts of different little treats in the city markets and old hamlets. Truth be told, it's something you can see all over the world, exception made for the "global" foods like burgers or *Kebab:* every city's got its own hidden gems to find. Ours come from simple, humble origins, where seconds were always welcome, where people appositely cooked more than they needed so that they could store the leftovers and use them again the next day. The hard worker who left home early, the little boy who went to school and came back in the afternoon... they usually brought things with them that we'd find in a pub or a deli, today. The classic calzone, the *pizzetta di pasta,* fried mozzarella, *timballo di maccheroni* or the even more traditional *cuzzetiello,* the closed end of a long bread loaf filled with meatballs or eggplant parmesan, that we can easily find on the street today. Due to the sheer competition between the many joints in the street food business, many old symbols like the *cuzzetiello,* the *tianiello* (a type of pasta) or the *cuoppo* (a cone of straw paper filled with different kinds of fried meat or fish) have been used in advertising to appeal to our pride.

In the following recipes, you'll find only salty foods, but it goes without saying that Neapolitan street food is rife with sweets, cookies or little desserts that you'll find in the other chapters of this book.

- Panino Napoletano *(Neapolitan Rolls)*
- Casatiello *(Neapolitan Stuffed Easter Bread)*
- Palle di riso al burro *(Rice balls with butter)*
- Crocchè di Patate *(Panzerotti)*
- Zeppole fritte *(Fried Zeppole)*
- Pizza al Trancio *(Sliced Pizza)*
- Pizza ripiena di scarole e salsicce *(Pizza stuffed with escarole and sausage)*
- Panino Friarielli e Salsicce *(Friarielli and Sausage Panini)*
- Panino Wurstel e Patatine *(Bockwurstel and chips panini)*
- Calzone Fritto *(Fried Calzone)*
- Pizza Fritta – Montanare *(Fried Pizza Dough with Tomato Sauce)*
- Frittata di Pasta *(Pasta Omelette)*
- Mozzarella in Carrozza *(Fried, breaded Mozzarella)*

Panino Napoletano (*Neapolitan Rolls*)

Let the yeast melt in water, then add sugar. reserve some of the water, to which you'll add salt later. Liberally flour the work surface, or stand mixer planetary with dough hook, you'll be using and start working the dough to incorporate air. Add water to the mixture and turn on the mixer at medium. Gradually add more water and increase the speed, until at the end you can add the salted water we kept aside before. Stir the dough until it sticks to the dough hook. If you do this by hand, then knead vigorously until the dough becomes smooth. Drizzle with oil and let it sit for a few hours, or until it doubles in size, wrapped in plastic. After two hours, spread the dough by patting it down on the countertop and fold it on itself a few times to strengthen the glutinic mesh. Shape the dough into a ball again, sprinkle some more oil and let it rest again for a few hours. Afterwards, roll it out by hand or with a rolling pin, until the dough becomes thin enough. Grease the surface with enough lard and cover it with the meat you diced beforehand, along with an hard-boiled egg, pepper and cheese to taste. carefully roll everything together and press lightly on top, in a shape reminiscent of a burrito. Cut the resulting roll in chunks of 3-4 centimeters each and set them in a baking tin with greaseproof paper, making sure they're spread evenly to favour leavening. Keep the tins covered, aired, and possibly warm, and let the rolls rest for at least an hour (or until they rise enough). gently brush some egg yolk on top and bake for 15-18 in a 180° Oven, always checking to make sure they're not burned.

Neapolitan rolls are like tiny casatielli with an added hard boiled egg, which is a tradition only seen in the city of Naples, not in the province, where casatielli are also called Tortani, due to a difference in ingredients.

INGREDIENTS

for about 20 sandwiches:

FOR THE DOUGH

- 500 GR MANITOBA FLOUR;
- 500 GR TYPE 00 FLOUR;
- ABOUT 550 ML WATER;
- 10 GR SUGAR;
- 25 GR BREWER'S YEAST;
- ½ CUP OIL;
- 20 GR SALT.

FOR THE FILLING

- 200 GR DICED PANCETTA;
- 200 GR DICED SALAME NAPOLI;
- 200 GR DICED HAM;
- 100 GR GRATED PECORINO;
- 3 DICED HARD-BOILED EGGS;
- 150 GR LARD;
- 2 EGG YOLKS;
- PEPPER TO TASTE.

Casatiello *(Neapolitan Stuffed Easter Bread)*

INGREDIENTS

FOR THE DOUGH

- 500 GR TYPE 00 FLOUR;
- 500 GR MANITOBA FLOUR;
- ABOUT 600 ML WATER;
- 20 GR SALT;
- 50 ML SEED OIL;
- 25 GR BREWER'S YEAST;
- 1 TSP. SUGAR;

FOR THE FILLING

- 150 GR LARD;
- 100 GR PECORINO CHEESE;
- 100 GR PARMESAN CHEESE;
- 500 GR DICED PANCETTA;
- 100 GR DICED SALAME NAPOLI;
- 50 GR CICOLI;
- PEPPER TO TASTE

TOPPINGS

- 3 EGGS;
- A LITTLE DOUGH.

Mix yeast, water and sugar in a bowl, but keep some water aside, to which you'll add salt later. Deliberately flour your work surface or stand mixer planetary with dough hook and start stirring the dough to incorporate some air. Gradually add water and oil and turn on the mixer at medium, gradually pour in more water and increase the speed, until at the end you'll add the salted water you reserved earlier. Stir the dough until it sticks to the hook. If you do this by hand, then knead vigorously until the dough becomes smooth. Drizzle with oil and let it sit for a few hours, or until it doubles in size, wrapped in plastic. After two hours, spread the dough by patting it down on the work surface and fold it on itself a few times to strengthen the glutinic mesh. Shape the dough into a ball again, sprinkle some more oil on it and let it rest again for a few hours. Afterwards, roll it out by hand or with a rolling pin, until the dough becomes thin enough. Grease the surface with enough lard and cover it with the meat you diced beforehand, along with an hard-boiled egg, pepper and cheese to taste.

Roll the dough, brushing it with a bit of lard on every fold. Once the filling is fully wrapped, be sure to tuck the two ends together, taking care not to break the dough. Liberally grease a tube pan with oil and place the dough inside. Be sure to choose a large enough pan, since the dough will rise to twice its height after resting. Place a few eggs randomly on top of the dough, making sure they're not fully submerged, using some leftover dough strands to make a cross over each egg. Place somewhere safe from the wind, covered with a cotton cloth.

After a few hours it should have risen to twice its initial height, and you can bake it in the oven at 180° for about an hour.

To make the casatiello a bit lighter and softer, let it bake with some water at the bottom of the oven for the first half hour, to make some steam. In the last ten minutes, open the oven door slightly to let the steam out: you will find that the crust around the casatiello has become rougher, while the inside is softer.

The story of the casatiello is as old as the Pastiera, and we can find proof of its use in 18th century books. This particular stuffed cake is a dear tradition in naples, and it's ubiquitous with easter, symbolizing many different facets of the christian holiday. Nowadays you can find it every time of the year in many bakeries or rotisseries, where it's sold in slices as a traditional-style street food.

* * *

Palle di riso al burro *(Rice balls with butter)*

Cook the rice in a large pot, dipping it completely in a mix of broth and saffron, but don't stir it. Let it soak up all the broth, then set aside. Mix in cheese and add salt and pepper, letting it cool down a bit to the point it can be safely shaped by hand.

Take a nice spoonful out and spread it on the palm of your hand, carving a little nook in the center. Fill that nook with a nub of butter and some diced mozzarella and ham; cover it with some more rice and roll it into a vague "orange" shape with a small tip on top. This is an essential step, because we have to make sure that the rice wrapping is filled up nicely.

Mix two parts water and one part flour in a cup until properly battered and add salt to taste. Coat the rice balls first in batter and then in dried bread crumbs. This will keep your rice ball properly "sealed" and avoid any spilling out during cooking. Deep fry the rice balls until brown, frying no more than a handful at the same time, dig them out and let the excess oil drain on some cooking paper. Serve hot or warm.

Arancini, as they're called in Sicily, or palle di riso,

INGREDIENTS
for about 10 rice balls

FOR THE RISOTTO

- 500 GR SEMI-WHOLE RICE;
- 30 GR BUTTER;
- 1 SACHET OF SAFFRON (ABOUT ¼ TEASPOON);
- 1 LT LIGHT BROTH;
- SALT AND PEPPER TO TASTE;
- 50 GR GRATED PARMESAN CHEESE.

FOR THE FILLING

- 100 GR DICED HAM;
- 100 GR PROVOLA OR MOZZARELLA STICKS;
- 50 GR BUTTER;
- TYPE 00 FLOUR;
- DRIED BREADCRUMBS Q.S.;
- SEED OIL FOR FRYING.

as we like to call them, are a bone fide main dish made with rice and different dressings (of which there are thousands in Sicily), like simple ham and mozzarella or classic ragù. You can eat it hot or warm, but it's delicious even when cold, wrapped in a sheet of straw paper while walking around the block.

* * *

Crocchè di Patate *(Panzerotti)*

INGREDIENTS

for about 20 panzerotti

- 1 KG STARCHY POTATOES, PREFERABLY YELLOW OR RED;
- 100 GR GRATED PECORINO;
- PARSLEY Q.S.;
- SALT AND PEPPER TO TASTE;
- 100 GR MOZZARELLA OR PROVOLA;
- 3 EGGS;
- FLOUR AND DRIED BREADCRUMBS Q.S.

Wash and boil the potatoes, only peeling them afterwards. Mash and then put inside a tin to cool. As soon as they're moderately cold, add each ingredient: yolks, parsley, pepper and pecorino. Roll a few handfuls of this mixture into a little ball, then flatten and put a strand of mozzarella or provola in the middle. Wrap everything up, shaping the mixture into a small sausage. Dip the panzerotto in flour, then in egg white and finally in dried breadcrumbs. Let them sit for a few hours in the fridge, and then deep fry them until they're a nice golden brown. Be sure to use starchy potatoes, preferably with a yellow paste, as they're perfect for this kind of recipe.

* * *

Zeppole fritte *(Fried Zeppole)*

INGREDIENTS

FOR THE DOUGH

- 250 GR TYPE 00 FLOUR;
- 200 ML WATER;
- 5 GR SALT;
- 25 GR BREWER'S YEAST;
- 1 TSP. SUGAR;
- PEPPER TO TASTE.

Melt the yeast in a cup of water, together with a teaspoon of sugar, and then mix with flour in a large bowl. Knead vigorously. The resulting dough has to be elastic enough to stick to an upside down spoon. Add the salt and continue kneading to mix. Let the dough rest until it is twice its original size.

Frying will require a tall pot filled with oil. Let it fry at 170° and dip a spoonful of dough in at a time (for as many times as the pot can carry). Always soak the spoon in water before using it, otherwise the dough will stick to it. Also, be careful not to let the water splash in the boiling oil.

We can add all kinds of different ingredients to the dough, but most have to be cooked first, like cauliflower, zucchini buds, algae, different seafood, etc.

When they've turned a light golden brown, fish them out of the pot and place them on a sheet of cooking paper. Serve hot with a sprinkle of salt.

* * *

Pizza al Trancio *(Sliced Pizza)*

Mix yeast, water and sugar in a bowl, keep some water aside and add salt to it. Liberally flour the work surface or stand mixer planetary with dough hook and start stirring the dough to incorporate some air. Gradually add water and oil and start the mixer at medium speed, then add some more water and increase speed gradually, until finally adding the salted water we set aside before. Stir the dough until it sticks to the hook. If you do this by hand, then knead vigorously until the dough becomes completely smooth. Drizzle with oil and let it rest for a few hours, or until it doubles in size, keeping it wrapped in plastic. After two hours, spread the dough by patting it down on the countertop and fold it on itself a few times to strengthen the glutinic mesh. Shape the dough into a ball again, sprinkle some more oil and let it rest again for a few hours. Afterwards, roll it out by hand or with a rolling pin, until it's about 1 cm thin. Grease a large oven tray with oil and place the dough on top. If it's too much, split it in half. Rest for another hour, and then put on the toppings: chunks of peeled tomatoes, mozzarella, basil, garlic, oil and salt.

These are only the "basic" toppings. You can add whatever you want, really. With or without tomatoes, with or without mozzarella, with veggies or meat or, god forbid, pineapple, pizza is always good.

Bake in a preheated oven, placed at the bottom so the surface doesn't dry up. If you notice the toppings drying, then cover the pizza with some tinfoil until done. Bake in a searing-hot 200° for 20 minutes. Cooking time can vary based on topping

INGREDIENTS

FOR THE DOUGH

- 500 GR TYPE 00 FLOUR;
- 500 GR MANITOBA FLOUR;
- ABOUT 600 ML WATER;
- 20 GR SALT;
- 50 ML SEED OIL;
- 25 GR BREWER'S YEAST;
- 1 TSP. SUGAR;

TOPPINGS

- 500 GR PEELED TOMATOES;
- 300 GR MOZZARELLA OR PROVOLA;
- 1 WHOLE GARLIC;
- 5/6 BASIL LEAVES;
- 2 TBSP. OIL;
- SALT AND PEPPER TO TASTE.

texture and quantity.

There's really not much left to be said about pizza: everybody's got their slice, even those who don't know a bag of flour from a shipment of baby powder. Maybe it's because it's an interesting, eye-catching topic. What's certain is that we can find pizza in every corner of the world, made in every which way: often with less than palatable results, sometimes a surprise, but a welcome one. I was lucky enough to be able to travel around the world, and to satisfy my own curiosity I sought out pizzerias both in the South of Italy, where even though the name remains the same the product is quite different, and the North, where it doesn't have a real "identity", but you can always find a helpful neighbourhood Southern immigrant who cooks it just like back home. Outside of our country, pizza explodes into different flavours and colours, mainly due to the fact that pizzerias are either run by immigrants or by locals who have learned their craft in Italy. "Our" pizza has her own distinct identity with very particular features: a thin texture, tall crust, made with the "classic" ingredients of our land.

* * *

Pizza ripiena di scarole e salsicce
(Pizza stuffed with escarole and sausage)

INGREDIENTS

FOR THE DOUGH

- 250 GR TYPE 00 FLOUR;
- 250 GR MANITOBA FLOUR;
- 300 ML WATER;
- 10 GR SALT;
- 30 ML SEED OIL;
- 25 GR BREWER'S YEAST;
- 1 TSP. SUGAR.

FOR THE FILLING

- 1 SMOOTH ESCAROLE;
- 100 GR BLACK OLIVES;
- A HANDFUL OF CAPERS;
- A HANDFUL OF RAISINS;
- A HANDFUL OF PINE NUTS;

Rinse the escarole, removing the central stem and outermost leaves. Blanch in a lidded pot without water for ten minutes. Combine a garlic clove, oil, a pinch of salt, a bit of chili in a pan and gently sautè for a while, then take off the heat.

In another pan, cook the sausages whole with a bit of water and oil, letting them simmer for about ten minutes.

Mix yeast, water and sugar in a bowl, keeping some water aside, to which you'll add salt later. Deliberately flour the countertop, or stand mixer planetary with dough hook you'll be using, and start stirring the dough to incorporate some air. Gradually add water and oil and start the mixer at medium speed, then add some more water and increase speed until adding the salted water we set aside before. Stir the dough until it sticks to the hook. If you do this by hand, then be forceful and knead until the dough becomes completely smooth. Drizzle with oil and let it rest for a few hours, or until it doubles in size, keeping it wrapped in plastic. After two hours, spread the dough by patting it down on the countertop and fold it on itself a few times to strengthen the glutinic mesh. Shape into a ball again, sprinkle with oil and let it rest. After about two hours, split the dough in half and roll out one half, either by hand or rolling pin, until it's about 1 cm thin. Put the thin dough in a tray greased with oil and top with escarole, sliced sausages, salt and pepper to taste, then set aside. Roll out the other half of the dough, making sure that it's the same size as the tray you prepared earlier, and cover the filling completely, sealing the corners and sides. Afterwards, lightly poke the central part of the pizza with a fork, making shallow holes for venting with the prongs.

Bake in a preheated oven at 180° for about 30/35 minutes.

* 2 TBSP. OIL;
* 1 CLOVE GARLIC;
* SALT TO TASTE;
* 4 PORK SAUSAGES.

* * *

Panino Friarielli e Salsicce
(Friarielli and Sausage Panini)

Rinse the friarielli and pluck the leaves from the stalk. Cook in a lidded pan without water for ten minutes, then add a garlic clove, oil, a pinch of salt, a bit of chili and gently sautè for a while. In another pan, cook the sausages whole with a bit of water and oil, letting them simmer for about ten minutes.

Mix yeast, water and sugar in a bowl, reserve some of the water to salt later. Deliberately flour the countertop, or stand mixer planetary with dough hook you'll be using, and start stirring the dough to incorporate some air. Gradually add water and oil and start the mixer at medium speed, then add

INGREDIENTS

FOR THE DOUGH

* 500 GR TYPE 00 FLOUR;
* 500 GR MANITOBA FLOUR;
* 550 ML WATER;
* ½ CUP OIL;
* 20 GR SALT;
* 25 GR BREWER'S YEAST;
* 1 TSP. SUGAR;

FOR THE FILLING

* 2 KG FRIARIELLI;
* 4 TBSP. OIL;
* 1 CLOVE GARLIC;
* 6 PORK SAUSAGES.

some more water and increase speed until adding the salted water we set aside before. Stir the dough until it sticks to the hook. If you do this by hand, then be forceful and knead until the dough becomes completely smooth. Drizzle with oil and let it rest for a few hours, or until it doubles in size, keeping it covered with a layer of cling film. After two hours, spread the dough by patting it down on the countertop and fold it on itself a few times to strengthen the glutinic mesh. Shape into a ball again, sprinkle with oil and let it rest. After about two hours, roll out the dough either by hand or rolling pin, until it's thin enough. Top with friarielli and diced sausage. Wrap the dough up in a roll, press lightly on top and close up the extremities. Cut the resulting roll in 3-4 cm long slices and place them on a tray with greaseproof paper, making sure they're evenly spread to let them rise. Keep the tray or trays in a dry, possibly warm place, and let them rest for about an hour, until they rise sufficiently, then brush with egg yolk. Bake for 15-18 minutes in a preheated oven at 180°, and always check to make sure they're not burning.

* * *

Panino Wurstel e Patatine
(Bockwurstel and chips panini)

INGREDIENTS

Dough for about 20 Panini:
- 500 GR TYPE 00 FLOUR;
- 500 GR MANITOBA FLOUR;
- 550 ML WATER;
- ½ CUP OIL;
- 20 GR SALT;
- 25 GR BREWER'S YEAST;
- 1 TSP. SUGAR;

FOR THE FILLING
- 20 BOCKWURST FRANKFURTERS;
- 1 KG POTATOES;
- FRYING OIL;
- SALT AND PEPPER TO TASTE.A HANDFUL OF PINE NUTS;

Mix yeast, water and sugar in a bowl, reserving some water to add salt in later. Liberally flour the work surface, or stand mixer planetary with dough hook you'll be using, and start stirring the dough to incorporate some air. Gradually add water and oil and start the mixer at medium speed, then add some more water and gradually increase speed, until finally adding the salted water we set aside before. Stir the dough until it sticks to the hook. If you do this by hand, then knead vigorously until the dough becomes completely smooth. Drizzle with oil and let it rest for a few hours, or until it doubles in size, keeping it covered with a layer of cling film. After two hours, spread the dough by patting it down on the work surface and fold it on itself a few times to strengthen the glutinic mesh. Ration the dough in many pieces of about 120 gr each, then roll each one into a ball and press lightly on top. Let them rest. After about two hours, fry in oil at 170°. Keep stirring until brown. remove from the pan and set on cooking paper. Rinse and peel the potatoes, cut them in thick slices and then in sticks, rinse again and drain (in a colander if you have one home). Cut the frankfurter in two or three pieces, and set up a pan to deep fry, first the potatoes and then the frankfurters. Cut the panini in half on one side and stuff them with chips and sausage, add a pinch of salt and pepper, and/or dip them in a sauce of your liking.

$$* * *$$

Calzone Fritto *(Fried Calzone)*

Mix yeast, water and sugar in a bowl, but keep some water aside, to which you'll add salt later. Liberally flour the work surface, or stand mixer planetary with dough hook you'll be using, and start stirring the dough to incorporate some air. Gradually add water and oil and start the mixer at medium speed, then add some more water and gradually increase speed, until finally adding the salted water we set aside before. Stir the dough until it sticks to the hook. If you do this by hand, then knead vigorously until the dough becomes completely smooth. Drizzle with oil and let it rest for a few hours, or until it doubles in size, keeping it wrapped in plastic. After two hours, spread the dough out by patting it down on the work surface and fold it on itself a few times to strengthen the glutinic mesh. Shape into a ball again, sprinkle with oil and let it rest. After a few hours, cut the dough in 50/60 gr chunks, roll each one into a ball and then flatten to form circles. Stuff with filling and close up. Set them on a lightly floured tray at an even distance from one another and let sit for at least an hour. Afterwards fry them in a pan at 170°, flipping them until both sides are

INGREDIENTS
for about 20 Calzones:

- 500 GR TYPE 00 FLOUR;
- 500 GR MANITOBA FLOUR;
- 600 ML WATER;
- 50 ML SEED OIL;
- 20 GR SALT;
- 25 GR BREWER'S YEAST;
- 1 TSP. SUGAR;

FOR THE FILLING

- 500 GR PROVOLA OR MOZZARELLA;
- 500 GR PEELED TOMATOES;
- 300 GR HAM;
- SALT AND PEPPER TO TASTE;

FILLING VARIATION

- 600 GR RICOTTA;
- 250 GR CICOLI;
- SALT AND PEPPER TO TASTE.

an even brown. The classic calzone filling is made of cicoli, ricotta, salt and pepper. Cicoli are little morsels of fat that melt into lard during cooking, with just a little squeeze.

In the years after the second world war, the rampant destruction and scarce financial means, mixed with a strong resolve to endure, led many street food businesses, most of them with humble origins and basic equipment, to rise and flourish in the alleys and squares of the city center. You didn't have to go far from home to find cooking stands with huge pots full of sizzling oil and all kinds of treats bubbling on the surface. A great testimony of this kind of activity can be found in the Vittorio de Sica movie "L'Oro di Napoli" ("The Gold of Naples"), where a young Sophia Loren plays the owner of a small "Neapolitan rotisserie", where she sells homemade fried food.

Pizza Fritta – Montanare
(Fried Pizza Dough with Tomato Sauce)

Mix yeast, water and sugar in a bowl, but reserve some water to add salt in later. Liberally flour the countertop, or stand mixer planetary with dough hook you'll be using, and start stirring the dough to incorporate some air. Gradually add water and oil and start the mixer at medium speed, then add some more water and gradually increase speed, until finally adding the salted water we set aside before. Stir the dough until it sticks to the hook. If you do this by hand, then knead vigorously until the dough becomes completely smooth. Drizzle with oil and let it rest for a few hours, or until it doubles in size, keeping it wrapped in plastic. After two hours, spread the dough by patting it down on the work surface and fold it on itself a few times to strengthen the glutinic mesh. Roll into a ball again, sprinkle with oil and let rest again. After a few hours, cut the dough in about 50/60 gr chunks. Roll each into a small ball and then pat it down in a full moon shape. Sprinkle some flour on a tray and place the discs at an even distance from each other. After about an hour, fry them in 170° hot oil. When they're done, place on a serving tray, top with tomatoes, mozzarella, basil, a handful of grated cheese and salt to taste. Serve immediately.

"Pizzette Fritte" are a centuries old neapolitan street food that used to be eaten daily by all the people coming and going on the city streets. The name "montanare" ("Mountaineers") comes from the fact that many city-bound country folk bought and ate this kind of fried pizza for lunch. Montanare were typically prepared by the wives of bakers, often using the leftover dough from the day before.

INGREDIENTS

FOR THE DOUGH

- 500 GR TYPE 00 FLOUR;
- 500 GR MANITOBA FLOUR;
- 600 ML WATER;
- 20 GR SALT;
- 50 ML SEED OIL;
- 25 GR BREWER'S YEAST;
- 1 TSP. SUGAR;

TOPPINGS

- 500 GR PEELED TOMATOES;
- 100 GR PECORINO CHEESE;
- 500 GR MOZZARELLA OR PROVOLA;
- 1 SMALL BUNCH BASIL, LEAVES PICKED;
- SALT AND PEPPER TO TASTE.

Frittata di Pasta *(Pasta Omelette)*

INGREDIENTS

for 5/6 people

- 500 GR PASTA (BUCATINI, ZITI, MACCHERONI OR MIXED);
- 6 EGGS;
- 1 LT BECHAMEL OR TOMATO SAUCE;
- 100 GR HAM;
- 200 GR SCAMORZA;
- 50 GR SALAME NAPOLI;
- 50 GR GRATED PECORINO CHEESE;
- 50 GR CHICKPEAS;
- SALT AND PEPPER TO TASTE.

Bring water and salt to boil in a large pot, then add the pasta and let it cook. Read the instructions on the pasta pack, remove and drain a few minutes before its given cooking time. Store in a large tin or baking dish. Add beaten eggs, béchamel or tomato sauce, cheese, diced ham, scamorza, cooked chickpeas, salt and pepper to taste. Give a good stir, and let all the flavors get to know each other.

Bring a drizzle of seed oil to a shimmer in a large saucepan. Tip in the pasta mixture we prepared before and cook on extremely low heat with the lid on. After about 10/15 minutes, check to see if the texture is firm enough to be inverted: there should be a thin crust on the bottom. Invert it with the help of the pan's lid (be careful not to break it!), and slow cook the other side for another 10 minutes. Stick a toothpick in to see if it's done, then slide it off the pan and serve warm on a platter.

Pasta Omelets was an inventive way for Neapolitan families to recycle the previous day's leftovers. Pasta, sauce and whatever else they could find were all mixed in a kind of casserole that was either cooked in the oven or fried, typically with very little oil and on really low heat. The modern version, common in rotisseries and restaurants, comes in small portions, often dipped in egg yolk and dried breadcrumbs.

Mozzarella in Carrozza *(Fried, breaded Mozzarella)*

Cut the stale bread in about 20 1 cm wide slices and then remove the crust. Slice the mozzarella, and mix beaten eggs with grated Parmigiano cheese, salt and pepper. Pour the milk in a bowl. Quickly dip the bread in milk and cover with a slice of mozzarella first, then another slice of bread. Gently squeeze the sandwich, then dip in egg batter first, and dried breadcrumbs soon after. Be sure to fully dip. Deep fry and serve immediately after cooking with a sprinkle of salt.

This delicious snack is the latest addition to the long list of "waste not, want not" food items, in this case using stale bread and leftover mozzarella.

INGREDIENTS
for 10 portions

- 20 SLICES OF STALE BREAD;
- 500 GR MOZZARELLA;
- 100 ML MILK;
- 4 EGGS;
- GRATED PARMIGIANO CHEESE;
- DRIED BREADCRUMBS;
- SALT AND PEPPER TO TASTE;
- FRYING OIL.

"To invite people to dine with us is to make ourselves responsible for their well-being for as long as they are under our roofs"

Anthelme Brillat-Savarin

Starters

"A chi me da 'o pane, ij o chiamm pat"

"Father is the one who gives me bread."

Neapolitan proverb

Starters

The French call starters "hors d'oeuvre", which roughly means "outside the main body of work"; this category is made of dishes that tickle the palate and entice your appetite: in essence, inviting food that's spread in many small, light portions. Outside of a restaurant's modus operandi, which is liable to kill you due to the sheer amount of stuff they serve for starters, a standard neapolitan lunch usually offers raw food, colorful salads, ground fish and/or meat dressed with oil or vinegar: dishes that don't overload your taste buds and stomach, and that aren't supposed to fill you up before the "work" starts. Different types of dairy products, meat and olives are always used as starters in a typical lunch.

- ZUCCHINE ALLA SCAPECE / *ESCABECHE (FRIED ZUCCHINI IN VINEGAR)*
- ALICI MARINATE *(MARINATED ANCHOVIES)*
- VERDURE ARROSTITE *(GRILLED VEGGIES)*
- FELLATA *(MEAT AND CHEESE PLATE)*
- INSALATA CAPRESE *(CAPRESE SALAD, WITH FRESH TOMATOES AND MOZZARELLA)*
- INSALATA DI POMODORI *(TOMATO SALAD)*
- FIOR DI ZUCCA IN PASTELLA *(FRIED PUMPKIN FLOWERS)*
- BRUSCHETTE *(GARLIC BREAD WITH TOMATOES)*
- INSALATA DI POLPO E PATATE *(OCTOPUS SALAD WITH POTATOES)*
- INSALATA DI MARE *(SEAFOOD SALAD)*

Zucchine alla Scapece / *Escabeche*
(Fried Zucchini in Vinegar)

INGREDIENTS

- 1 KG ZUCCHINI;
- 1 BUNCH OF MINT;
- 150 ML RED WINE VINEGAR;
- 150 ML WATER;
- SALT AND PEPPER TO TASTE;
- ½ CLOVE GARLIC;

TO FRY

- EVO OIL, Q.S.

Rinse and trim the ends of the zucchini then slice into rounds about 3-4mm thick. Place them in a colander or a wire rack and season with salt. Let sit for about an hour to drain the excess vegetable water. Afterwards, rinse quickly in the sink and then dry with kitchen paper. Fry the zucchini in medium heat olive oil until brown, then drain on kitchen paper. In a saucepan, combine vinegar, half a garlic clove, water and some mint leaves and boil for ten minutes.

Place the zucchini in a shallow bowl, layered on top of one another with a little mint and pepper in between. Sprinkle with the vinegar you boiled before. Wrap the bowl in plastic and marinate for at least 24 hours before serving. When ready, remove the film, pluck however many zucchini you need and serve on a plate with a sprinkle of oil.

The So-called scapece is a marinating process used for different ingredients that are first fried in olive oil, and then marinated in a mixture of vinegar, water and spices. It was originally an Arabian technique, but it was perfected in Spain. In the movie "Il Turco Napoletano" by acclaimed Neapolitan actor and comedian Totò, villain and resident neighborhood bully Don Carluccio "Man of Steel" (interpreted by actor Enzo Turco) mentions this delicious dish in his pre-nuptial contract among a comically long list of foods he dislikes, referring to them by their original Neapolitan name: cocozzielli alla scapece.

Alici marinate *(Marinated Anchovies)*

Wash the anchovies, cut off the head and remove the entrails, then slit each fish vertically from "head" to tail, using a sharp paring knife or even only your thumb if you're feeling wild (that's the traditional way). Carefully pull out the spine. Rinse under running tap water and place in a tall bowl, then douse in vinegar until fully covered and marinate for ¾ hours. Afterwards, drain the vinegar and sprinkle with oil, garlic, chili, salt and pepper to taste. Let all the tastes get to know each other for a few hours, then serve.

INGREDIENTS

- 500 GR FRESH ANCHOVIES;
- 50 ML RED WINE VINEGAR;
- 1 GARLIC CLOVE;
- 100 ML EVO OIL;
- A SPRIG OF PARSLEY;
- SALT AND PEPPER TO TASTE.

* * *

Verdure Arrostite *(Grilled Veggies)*

Rinse the veggies, then trim the ends of the zucchini and slice them lengthwise. Cut off the eggplant stem and also slice vertically. Peel the onions and tranche in rounds. Remove the pumpkin's hard outer skin and sliver in 3-4mm thick slices, then finally cut the tomatoes in thick rounds.

Preheat a cast iron grill for about ten minutes, place the veggies on top and flip them only when they don't stick to the surface anymore. Once flipped, let them cook on the other side too, then remove them immediately afterwards and place on a platter. Top with garlic, chili, oregano, mint and salt, oil and balsamic vinegar.

INGREDIENTS

- 2 MEDIUM ZUCCHINI;
- 2 MEDIUM EGGPLANTS;
- 2 MEDIUM PEPPERS;
- 1 LARGE RED ONION;
- 1 PIECE OF PUMPKIN;
- 2 TOMATOES;
- GARLIC;
- EVO OIL;
- SALT TO TASTE;
- CHILI;
- BALSAMIC VINEGAR;
- OREGANO;
- MINT.

* * *

Fellata *(Meat and Cheese Plate)*

Slice salame and capocollo, cut the cheese in sticks and the eggs in rounds. Place all the different ingredients on a platter or a wooden tray, alternating between meat, cheese and eggs. If you like, you can serve together with small sauce or honey ramekins filled with cheese, celery sticks for the meat, accompanied by bruschettas.

INGREDIENTS

- 200 GR SALAME NAPOLI;
- 200 GR CAPOCOLLO;
- 300 GR CACIOCAVALLO;
- 200 GR SALTED RICOTTA;
- 300 GR PROVOLONE;
- 4 HARD-BOILED EGGS.

Insalata Caprese
(Caprese Salad, with fresh tomatoes and mozzarella)

INGREDIENTS

- 500 GR CAMPANIAN BUFFALO MOZZARELLA;
- 4 RIPE SORRENTO TOMATOES;
- 10 BASIL LEAVES;
- EVO OIL Q.S.;
- SALT TO TASTE

Slice the mozzarella and drain the milk in a plate for half an hour. Cut the tomatoes in slices and place them in a platter, then layer with mozzarella and basil leaves, in a full circle. Sprinkle with EVO oil and salt. Let all the tastes mesh together for a few minutes before serving, until the oil has trickled down deep enough.

One of the best excellences of Campania, our buffalo mozzarella is famous all over the world, and I chose Sorrento Tomatoes for this recipe since they have a more fitting taste and shape than other (equally as good) Campanian varieties. Caprese is a simple recipe to prepare quickly and easily, but it can be made delicious with the right oil and fresh basil. As said before in the opening chapters, the production of Mozzarella is spread all over the Campanian territory, and goes well beyond the "classic" buffalo mozzarella. the area of Cilento in southern Campania offers many different cheeses and dairy products, like the famous "Zizzona" (quite literally, "the big tiddy", for its... peculiar shape). Agerola and Aversa also boast a centuries-old agricultural tradition, whose provola, provolone, Ricotta and Scamorza are the pride and joy of many farmers in the area.

Speaking of mozzarella, I'm reminded of an iconic scene from a beloved neapolitan movie, "Miseria e Nobiltà", directed in the mid-fifties by Mario Mattoli and adapted from a play by neapolitan playwright Mario Scarpetta. Enzo Turco asks his friend Totò to pawn his vest, just to put food on the table at lunch. "So, you buy about a pound of Aversan mozzarella, extra fresh! And make sure it's good: pinch it with your index and thumb, and if milk comes out, you buy it, if not, forget about it!"

Insalata di Pomodori *(Tomato Salad)*

Rinse and dry the tomatoes, cut in slices about half a centimeter thick and place on a platter. Layer on top of one another, radially from the center. Sliver the onions in rounds and place them on top of the tomatoes. Mince garlic and basil, then sprinkle on top along with salt and pepper to taste. Place the olives in the center, then drizzle oil on top. Wait a few minutes before serving.

INGREDIENTS

for 4/5 people

- 500 GR SORRENTO TOMATOES;
- 6/7 FRESH BASIL LEAVES;
- 4 TBSP. EVO OIL;
- 1 CLOVE GARLIC;
- 1 RED TROPEA ONION;
- 100 GR GREEN OLIVES;
- SALT AND PEPPER TO TASTE.

* * *

Fior di Zucca in Pastella *(Fried Pumpkin Flowers)*

Prepare the batter by mixing water, flour, yeast and salt in a bowl. Vigorously work the batter until it's soft enough. In a little pot boil some water and quickly dip the flowers one by one, after cutting off the stem.

Let the batter rest for about an hour, then bring a pan to 170° heat with enough oil. Using a fork, batter up a pumpkin flower, and place in the pan to fry. Do the same for every other flower. Stir until brown. As soon as they're ready, drain on cooking paper and serve hot with a sprinkle of salt and pepper.

INGREDIENTS

- 12/15 PUMPKIN FLOWERS;
- 300 GR FLOUR;
- 300 ML WATER;
- 12 GR BREWER'S YEAST;
- SALT AND PEPPER TO TASTE;
- FRYING OIL.

* * *

Bruschette *(Garlic Bread with Tomatoes)*

Cut the bread in about 1cm thick slices. Slice and dice the tomatoes with a sharp paring knife, then place into a bowl and combine with minced garlic, onion and basil. Drizzle with oil, add salt and pepper, then let all the tastes come together for a while.

Toast the bread on a cast iron plate or in the oven, making sure to flip regularly until uniformly brown. Place the bruschetta on a platter and gently rub the cut side of a half clove of garlic on it, to

INGREDIENTS

for 4/5 People

- 300 GR FRESH OR STALE BREAD;
- 500 GR SORRENTO TOMATOES;
- 6/7 FRESH BASIL LEAVES;
- 4 TBSP. EVO OIL;
- 1 GARLIC CLOVE;
- 1 RED TROPEA ONION;
- SALT AND PEPPER TO TASTE.

season. Give one last shake to the tomato mixture, then use a spoon to top each bruschetta. Drizzle with oil, and they're ready to serve!

The Sorrento Tomato is a product that's originally farmed around the Sorrento Peninsula, even though many other places in the Vesuvius range grow it too, these days. It's a decently-sized tomato, round in shape, ribbed and rosy-red in colour, with hints of green immediately after harvesting. It's a true delicacy, perfect to make salads like the caprese or used as a bruschetta topping. Having some means giving that little bit more taste we need for our dish, but other kinds of tomatoes with similar features are perfectly fine.

✳ ✳ ✳

Insalata di Polpo e Patate
(Octopus Salad with Potatoes)

INGREDIENTS

- ONE 1KG OCTOPUS;
- 700 GR POTATOES;
- 3 TBSP. OIL;
- 1 CLOVE GARLIC;
- 1 SPRIG PARSLEY;
- A HANDFUL OF CAPERS;
- 1 LEMON;
- SALT TO TASTE.

Wash and clean the octopus, cut off the eyes and mouth, eviscerate the sac and rinse under running tap water. Fill a pot with about 3 cm water and bring to boil. Holding the octopus by the sac, dip the tentacles in and out for a few times until they curl, after which immerse completely, close the lid and cook for about twenty minutes. turn off the heat, and let the octopus simmer in its own water for about half an hour. If you don't want the red outer skin to peel off, add some ice in the water before you pull it out. After taking it out, let it cool down for a few minutes and cut into large pieces, which you will put in a bowl of your choosing. blanch the potatoes in a pot with abundant water, filled to cover them. Let them boil for about 20 minutes, even though time may vary based on the potatoes' size. You can check their readiness with the prongs of a fork: they should slide in easily, once they're done. When they're ready, cool under running tap water, peel and dice roughly. Wait for them to get a bit colder and then combine with the diced Octopus. Dress with minced garlic and parsley, add garlic and drizzle with oil. Stir a bit to let everything come together, and serve garnished with lemon slices.

Insalata di Mare *(Seafood Salad)*

Wash and clean the octopus, cut off the eyes and mouth, eviscerate the sac and rinse under running tap water. Fill a pot with about 3 cm water and bring to boil. Holding the octopus by the sac, dip the tentacles in and out for a few times until they curl, after which immerse completely, close the lid and cook for about twenty minutes. turn off the heat, and let the octopus simmer in its own water for about half an hour. If you don't want its red outer skin to peel off, add some ice in the water before you pull it out. After taking it out, let it cool down for a few minutes and cut into large pieces, which you will put in a bowl of your choosing. Clean out the calamari and cuttlefish viscera from their sacs and remove the eyes, mouth and the bone or fin from their shell. Dice and boil, like you did with the octopus above. As soon as they're ready, cool and combine with the diced octopus. Clean the mussels of all impurities inside the shell, cut out the byssus, and place them in a pan with shallow water. Close the lid and wait for them to open up. Pluck them from their shell and place in the bowl along with the other seafood. Do the same with the clams. Clean the shrimp, cut off their head, rinse under running tap water and boil for about 5 minutes. Drain and cool, then peel and mix with the other seafood. Finally, roughly mince some parsley, celery and garlic and mix in the bowl along with capers and olives. Sprinkle some oil and salt, and serve with a lemon wedge.

INGREDIENTS

for 8/10 People

- ONE 1 KG OCTOPUS;
- 2 MEDIUM CALAMARI;
- 2 MEDIUM CUTTLEFISH;
- 500 GR MEDIUM SHRIMP;
- 500 GR CLAMS;
- 1 KG MUSSELS;
- 3 TBSP. OIL;
- 1 CLOVE GARLIC;
- 1 SPRIG PARSLEY;
- A HANDFUL OF CAPERS;
- 200 GR BLACK OLIVES;
- 1 CELERY STALK;
- SALT TO TASTE.

"Nobody is known to have seduced another with what they already offered to eat, but there's a long list of people who seduced others by explaining what they were about to serve"

Manuel Vazquez Montalban

Pasta Dishes

"A meglio mericina: vino, campagna, purpette e cucina"

"The best medicine: good wine, open country, and meatballs in the pot"

Neapolitan proverb

Pasta Dishes

To my utmost regret, the idea of a first course the way I like it, which means a nice, saucy pasta dish, is a bit passé. We're all on a constant diet, now. We give carbs the stink-eye, and don't particularly like heavy oils and other similarly caloric ingredients. Let me tell you, though: no diet survives contact with a well-made *pasta al dente*.

The midday lunch, together with a robust breakfast, provided the fuel for a day of hard manual labour and a work-intensive, yet decidedly less hectic, social life, without any means of transport except for one's very own feet. Thus the carbs-and-fats-heavy meals of the past thinned down a lot with the passing of time, as our activities became more and more sedentary, but they still provide plenty of sustenance in an ever-dieting world.

- Pasta e Fagioli *(Pasta and Beans)*
- Pasta e Ceci *(Pasta and Chickpeas)*
- Pasta e Lenticchie *(Pasta and Lentils)*
- Pasta e Patate con la Provola *(Pasta with Potatoes and Provola)*
- Lasagna
- Cannelloni *(Pasta filled with Ragù)*
- Sartù di Riso *(Rice Timbale)*
- Gnocchi alla Sorrentina
  (Sorrento-Style Gnocchi, with tomato sauce and mozzarella)
- Spaghetti a Vongole *(Clam Spaghetti)*
- Spaghetti alla Puttanesca "Aulive e Chiappiariell"
  (Spaghetti Puttanesca, with Tomato Sauce, Olives and Capers)
- Spaghetti Aglio e Oglio *(Spaghetti with Oil and Garlic)*
- Rigatoni al Ragù *(Rigatoni with Ragù)*
- Risotto alla Pescatora *(Seafood Risotto)*
- Pasta e Cucozza *(Pumpkin Pasta)*
- Pasta e Cavolo (Cauliflower Pasta)
- Paccheri ai Frutti di Mare *(Seafood Paccheri)*
- Spaghetti del Poverello *(Spaghetti with Egg, Cheese and Pepper)*
- Spaghetti ai Polpi *(Octopus Spaghetti)*
- Spaghetti alla Pizzaiola *(Spaghetti with Tomato Sauce and Oregano)*
- Rigatoni alla Genovese
  (Rigatoni Genovese, with Onions and Ground Meat)
- Pasta Fagioli e Cozze *(Pasta with Beans and Mussels)*

Pasta e Fagioli *(Pasta and Beans)*

INGREDIENTS

for 4/5 People

- 500 GR DRIED CANNELLINI BEANS;
- A PINCH OF BAKING SODA;
- 400 GR MIXED PASTA OR DITALONI (BIG, GROOVED THIMBLES)
- 1 TBSP. EVO OIL;
- 1 CLOVE GARLIC;
- 1 MEDIUM ONION;
- 1 CARROT;
- 1 CELERY STALK;
- 4/5 RED CHERRY TOMATOES;
- 1 LAUREL LEAF;
- 2/3 PARMESAN CHEESE RINDS;
- 1 PIECE CHOPPED PORK RIND;
- SALT TO TASTE.

In a large pot mix water and a pinch of baking soda, add the beans and let them rest overnight. The next day rinse them under running tap water and then cook together with a laurel leaf for about 40 minutes, leaving them to soak in their own water afterwards. In a saucepan, mix the whole garlic with oil, carrot, finely-diced onion and celery, the chopped pork rind and salt to taste. Add a bit of chili if you're feeling saucy. Sauté for about ten minutes, remove the garlic from the pan and add the tomatoes, chopped in half, then about 2/3 of the beans. Reserve 1/3 to blend with a kitchen mixer, then combine with the tomato-beans sauce and cook for about 20 minutes, mixing in some of the beans' own water. At this point, it's time to cook the pasta in the sauce you're preparing: make sure that the water is about level with the amount of pasta you're using, add some if it's too dry. A few minutes before the pasta is ready, mix in the Parmesan cheese rinds and salt to taste, checking that the water level is to your taste: some people like it a bit soupier, while others a little creamier (also consider it's going to take a few more minutes to be ready). Once it's done, taste to see if the pasta's cooked the way you like it, then turn off the heat, put on the lid and wait a few minutes before serving.

The whole peninsula is rife with legume-based dishes, and yet the Mezzogiorno is particularly rich in this type of cuisine, usually accompanied with a side of bread or pasta: most farmers used to enjoy this meal to get a carbs-induced second wind while toiling in the fields. every pasta dish or soup we have today are characteristic of a specific territory, with its local ingredients. Here in Campania, we generally mix tomatoes, pork rind, chili pepper, spices and aromas of our land, often picked in the wild, to make our own pasta e fagioli. I believe that what makes this recipe really "ours" is the fact that the pasta and the other ingredients have to "stick together", that means with little water, thick in texture, to the point you could scoop it up with a fork.

Pasta e Ceci *(Pasta and Chickpeas)*

Combine water and baking soda in a large pot, and soak the chickpeas for a whole night. The following day, rinse under running tap water and then boil with a sprig of rosemary for about 50 minutes. Let them rest in their own water. In a saucepan, mix garlic, oil, carrot, finely chopped celery, tomatoes and a little chili, if you like. Sauté for 10/15 minutes, pluck the garlic out, then mix in 2/3 of the chickpeas, reserving the last part to blend with a kitchen mixer and add in the mixture a bit later. Let everything cook for about 20 minutes, adding some of the chickpeas' cooking liquid to taste. At this point, it's time to actually cook the pasta in the sauce you're preparing: make sure that the water is about level with the amount of pasta you're using; add some if it's too dry. A few minutes before the pasta is ready, mix in the Parmesan cheese rinds and add salt, checking that the water level is to your taste: some people like it a bit soupier, while others a little creamier (also consider that it's going to take a few more minutes to be ready). Once it's done, taste to see if the pasta's cooked the way you like it, then turn off the heat, put on the lid and wait a few minutes before serving.

INGREDIENTS
for 4/5 People:

- 500 GR CHICKPEAS;
- 400 GR MIXED PASTA;
- ½ TSP. BAKING SODA;
- 1 TSP. EVO OIL;
- 1 MEDIUM ONION;
- 1 CARROT;
- 1 CELERY STALK;
- 4/5 RED CHERRY TOMATOES;
- 1 BUNCH ROSEMARY;
- 2 PARMESAN CHEESE RINDS;
- SALT TO TASTE.

* * *

Pasta e Lenticchie *(Pasta and Lentils)*

Rinse the lentils under running tap water and boil them with a laurel leaf for about 20 minutes, then remove the laurel leaf and let them rest in their own water. In a saucepan, combine garlic, oil, a diced potato, finely chopped parsley, tomatoes (cut in half), salt and a bit of chili, if you're feeling spicy. Sauté for about 10/15 minutes, remove the garlic, mix in the lentils and continue cooking for about 15 minutes, adding in a bit of their cooking liquid. it's time to cook the pasta in the sauce you're preparing: make sure that the water is about level with the amount of pasta you're using. Stir every once in

INGREDIENTS
for 4/5 People

- 400 GR DRIED LENTILS;
- 400 GR SPAGHETTI;
- 1 TBSP. EVO OIL;
- 1 CLOVE GARLIC;
- 1 POTATO;
- 1 SPRIG PARSLEY;
- 4/5 RED CHERRY TOMATOES;
- 1 LAUREL LEAF;
- SALT TO TASTE.

a while and add salt, checking that the water level is to your taste: some people like it a bit soupier, while others a little creamier (also consider that it's going to take a few more minutes to be ready). Once it's done, taste to see if the pasta's cooked the way you like it, then turn off the heat, put on the lid and wait a few minutes before serving.

Pasta e Lenticchie is one of the traditional Neapolitan dishes that we still enjoy often. It's a quick and easy recipe that brings out the delicious taste of this legume, which means it's rarely left out of weekday meals. It needs to be said that we don't make pasta with it as often as we used to: today we tend to favor even quicker recipes like lentil soup, or even salad.

* * *

Pasta e Patate con la Provola
(Pasta with Potatoes and Provola)

INGREDIENTS

for 5/6 People

- 500 GR MIXED PASTA;
- 400 GR POTATOES;
- 2 TSP. EVO OIL;
- ½ ONION;
- 50 GR SMOKED PANCETTA;
- 1 CELERY STALK;
- 250 GR PROVOLA;
- 50 GR GRATED PECORINO CHEESE;
- SALT AND PEPPER TO TASTE.

Clean and peel the potatoes, then roughly dice, rinse under running tap water and drain. In a saucepan mix oil, pancetta, chopped onion and celery and sauté for 10 minutes, after which cut the tomatoes in half and add them in, along with diced potatoes and salt, and cook for another 10 minutes. Once everything is sufficiently sautéed, add a few cups of water and let everything stew for 20/25 minutes more. Now it's time to cook the pasta: make a mental note of how much water you need, then pour it in the sauce and wait until boiling point to add the pasta. Let it cook until al dente, or a bit more if you like, and at the end mix in the diced provola, grated pecorino, salt and pepper to taste. Stir until the provola melts completely. Put the lid on and stew a little more before serving.

One of the first iterations of this recipe can be found in an old handwritten cookbook from 1773, "Il Cuoco galante (The Gentleman Cook)" by Vincenzo Corrado. This dish has seen a resurgence lately: many recent additions like the provola, or the technique of cooking it inside little terracotta tins, are only flairs for a dish that is, in origin, very humble, but always tastes great.

Lasagna

Neapolitan lasagna is slightly different from standard Italian lasagna, which means it's prepared with similar base ingredients, but ones that are closely tied to our cuisine. the sauce we'll be using is the quintessential Neapolitan Ragù, with a topping of the same meat we use for the sauce and tiny meatballs. For the recipe of ragù and meatballs, please check recipe #12 ("Rigatoni al Ragù") of this chapter, and recipe #10 ("Polpette") of chapter 5.

Take a tall oven tray of about 40 x 20 cm, since a standard portion is about 10 x 10 cm. Some quick math later, and you're left with 8 nice, generous servings. Begin by spreading sauce on the bottom of the tray, then carefully cover with lasagna noodles, making sure that it's about 1 cm away from the border, since it will grow slightly in the oven. Then top (in this order) with more sauce, minced meat, lightly-fried tiny meatballs, all the different types of cheese and a pinch of salt and pepper. Continue layering until you reach the top of the tray, which should be about three more layers of pasta. Spread ragù and cheese on top (avoid topping with minced meat as it will only get dry and flaky in the oven), liberally sprinkle with cheese, a pinch of salt as you did for the bottom layers, and then bake for 50/60 minutes in a preheated oven at 180°. Check during this time to make sure the sauce doesn't dry up, then turn off the oven and leave it inside (with the oven door slightly open) for about 20 minutes.

INGREDIENTS

for 8/10 People

- 500 GR FRESH LASAGNA NOODLES;
- 2 LT. POT OF TRADITIONAL NEAPOLITAN RAGÙ;
- 1 KG MIXED GROUND MEAT ("MEATBALL MIXTURE");
- 250 GR MOZZARELLA;
- 250 GR PROVOLA;
- 100 GR PARMESAN CHEESE;
- 100 GR PECORINO CHEESE;
- 250 GR SHEEP'S MILK RICOTTA;
- SALT TO TASTE.

Cannelloni *(Pasta filled with Ragù)*

INGREDIENTS

for 30 Cannelloni

- 1 BOX CANNELLONI ALL' UOVO;
- 2 LT. POT OF TRADITIONAL NEAPOLITAN RAGÙ;
- 300 GR GROUND FRESH LEAN BEEF;
- 300 GR GROUND LEAN PORK;
- 2 CARROTS;
- 1 ONION;
- 1 SMALL CELERY STICK;
- 4 TBSP. EVO OIL;
- ½ CUP RED WINE;
- 300 GR SHEEP'S MILK RICOTTA;
- 200 GR MOZZARELLA;
- 200 GR PROVOLA;
- 10 FRESH BASIL LEAVES;
- 50 GR GRATED PARMESAN CHEESE;
- SALT AND PEPPER TO TASTE.

Once again, follow the instructions on recipe #12 ("Rigatoni al Ragù") to prepare the ragù for this dish.

In a large saucepan, mix finely minced carrot, onion and celery, and sauté in oil for about 5 minutes. Tip in the ground beef, deglaze with a half cup of red wine, then turn off the heat.

Cut mozzarella and provola in small pieces, then soften up the ricotta with a spoonful of ragù. Pour the sautéed meat, mozzarella, provola, ricotta, cheese, salt and pepper in a bowl then give everything a good stir. Fill the cannelloni with this mixture, taking care not to break them apart. Spread sauce on the bottom of a standard oven tray, then place the cannelloni on top until the sauce is fully covered. Add another layer of ragù, which you will dilute with water in case it's too thick. Sprinkle with cheese, grated basil and a pinch of salt. Bake in a preheated 180° oven for at least 40 minutes, always checking to make sure the sauce hasn't dried up. Serve with a sprinkle of ragù and top with grated cheese.

A similar dish is mentioned once again by our dear Vincenzo Corrado in his book "Il Cuoco Galante": he writes about cooking a stuffed "pacchero", a type of pasta that's very similar to the cannelloni we traditionally prepare around Mardi Gras. Cannelloni are loved the world over, along with their big sister, the Lasagna, which Neapolitans also prepare in time for "Carnevale". During busy days in restaurant chains from abroad, a plate of cannelloni or lasagna is always in the fridge, ready to be served.

Sartù di Riso *(Rice Timbale)*

Third time's the charm, so I urge you to check the recipe for ragù (#12 of this chapter "Rigatoni al Ragù") and meatballs (#10, Chapter 5 "Polpette"), both essential ingredients of a good *sartù*. Prepare the ragù sauce and the ground meat, which you will roll into little balls and fry lightly, then set aside for later. Boil the eggs for about 9/10 minutes, then cool under running tap water and shell them. Dice mozzarella and provola, grate the parmesan cheese. While everything is getting nice and warm, cook the rice in the ragù sauce, adding about a cup of water. If this isn't your first time, and you're feeling confident about it, you can cook the rice without stirring it: it will be ready once it's absorbed all the liquid.

Once ready, season with salt, cheese and pepper.

Butter a bundt pan (baking dish with raised edges and a hole in the middle) and coat with dried breadcrumbs first, and the rice second, making sure you leave a little cavity in the center. Cover with meatballs, mozzarella, provola, hard-boiled egg wedges and a handful of peas. Layer rice and filling until you reach the top of the pan. Top with another layer of rice and dried breadcrumbs.

Bake in a preheated oven at 180° for at least 40 minutes. When it's done. take it out of the oven and let it cool for at least an hour. Flip it out of the pan onto a large platter or serving tray.

Serve sliced and topped with a spoonful of hot ragù and a sprinkle of grated parmesan cheese.

Our people always had a special term for rice: "Sciacquapanza", which roughly means "bowel cleaner". You may guess that rice has never really been a culinary sensation in Naples, despite being imported in Italy as early as 1600, and it was only really used in hospitals to treat intestinal dysfunctions, hence the name. We owe King Ferdinand IV, or more accurately

INGREDIENTS
for 7/8 People

- 1,5 LT. RAGÙ SAUCE;
- 500 GR MIXED GROUND BEEF ("MEATBALL MIXTURE");
- 500 GR CARNAROLI RICE;
- 2 HARD-BOILED EGGS;
- 100 GR CANNED PEAS;
- 250 GR MOZZARELLA;
- 250 GR PROVOLA;
- 50 GR GRATED PARMESAN CHEESE;
- SALT AND PEPPER TO TASTE.

his wife Marie Caroline of Austria, for the "invention" of sartù: the queen never really liked Neapolitan food, so the king summoned some French chefs to court and had them come up with a way to make the readily-available rice more palatable to his spouse; the resulting dish was, against all odds, a great success, and it remains a favourite among Neapolitans even today.

* * *

Gnocchi alla Sorrentina

(Sorrento-Style Gnocchi, with tomato sauce and mozzarella)

INGREDIENTS
for 5/6 people

FOR THE GNOCCHI:

- 1 KG TYPE 00 FLOUR;
- 400 GR POTATOES;
- 1 EGG;
- SALT TO TASTE.

FOR THE SAUCE:

- 2 750 ML BOTTLES
OF TOMATO SAUCE;
- 1 GARLIC CLOVE;
- 4/5 FRESH BASIL LEAVES;
- 250 GR PROVOLA;
- 250 GR MOZZARELLA;
- 50 GR PARMESAN CHEESE;
- 50 GR PECORINO CHEESE;
- SALT AND PEPPER TO TASTE.

Clean and boil the potatoes, making sure not to overcook them since they'd be soaking in too much water. Drain, peel, then mash with a potato masher. Wait until cool and quickly mix them with egg and flour, until you get a few "sticks" of dough, which you will cut, sprinkling with flour as needed, into small pieces. You can use the prongs of a fork to shape the dough in grooved curls, but if you still haven't learned how to do that, it's alright.

Prepare the sauce by gently heating the garlic in oil, letting it soften but not colour, then remove it and pour the tomato sauce in. add the basil leaves and salt, and cook for about an hour. Dice mozzarella and provola, grate the cheese. Bring a pot of water to boil and tip the gnocchi in. Keep them in just enough to heat them, they should still feel thick and not springy when you pull them out. Drain quickly, then mix in the same pot with abundant sauce, about 2/3 of the mozzarella and provola, cheese and some basil leaves. Place in a sauce-coated baking tin with raised edges, then top with the remaining mozzarella, provola and cheese. Sprinkle with pepper and salt to taste, then bake in a pre-heated oven for about 20 minutes (180°).

Serve hot, straight out of the oven.

We can find traces of the "gnocco" all over Italy, as far back as the 17th century. In Naples, it seemed to be especially liked by nobles, who had it prepared for wedding receptions and military parades. The Sorren-

to-style gnocchi were born in the Sorrento peninsula, where they paired the gnocchi with pizza ingredients (tomatoes, mozzarella and basil), serving them in the characteristic "Pignatiello", a small ceramic or terracotta bowl.

This dish, too, is often a choice pick for many menus, in restaurants all around the world.

* * *

Spaghetti a Vongole *(Clam Spaghetti)*

Clean the clams well, then place in a saucepan with a half cup of water, put the lid on and cook for 5/6 minutes until they open up, then drain and set the water aside for later use, filtering it through a strainer. In a pan filled with oil, gently heat the garlic until softened, then remove it. cut the cherry tomatoes into wedges and remove the seeds, then mix in the pan with the chili powder, half the parsley sprig, and clams. Add just a bit of clam cooking water, and sauté for about 5/6 minutes. Bring a pot of water to boil, and tip in the pasta as soon as it reaches boiling point. Cook until about two minutes before given cooking time, then drain and add to the pan, along with the remaining clam cooking water you set aside earlier. Sauté for another two minutes, while continuously stirring and tossing the pasta. Taste for seasoning and salt as needed. Add the remaining parsley in, drizzle with raw EVO Oil and serve, using a ladle and fork to twist the spaghetti into a small mound. Top with a bit of sauce and some clams.

Spaghetti alle vongole are a must in Neapolitan cuisine, so easy and quick to make that you could set up the table, prepare the sauce and boil the water at the same time. It only takes a scant few ingredients to make, even the tomatoes are optional, but the resulting sea aroma permeates the whole house and excites the palate with its unrivaled taste.

INGREDIENTS
for 5/6 People

- 1 KG MIXED CLAMS*;
- 600 GR SPAGHETTI;
- 1 CLOVE GARLIC;
- 2 TBSP. EVO OIL;
- 7/8 RED CHERRY TOMATOES;
- 1 SMALL BUNCH PARSLEY;
- SALT TO TASTE;
- A PINCH OF CHILI POWDER.

---

*CLAMS for the sake of tradition, we'll be using two local variants called lupini and vongole veraci, but you can use whatever you have available in your markets.

Spaghetti alla Puttanesca "Aulive e Chiappiariell"
(Spaghetti Puttanesca, with Tomato Sauce, Olives and Capers)

INGREDIENTS
for 5/6 People

- 500 GR SPAGHETTI OR LINGUINE;
- 400 GR CHERRY TOMATOES (DATTERINI);
- 2 TBSP. EVO OIL;
- 1 CLOVE GARLIC;
- 1 SMALL BUNCH PARSLEY;
- 50 GR CAPERS;
- 250 GR BLACK OLIVES;
- SALT TO TASTE.

Rinse and stone the olives. In a large pan, heat the garlic in oil until soft, then remove. Sauté parsley and capers for a few minutes, then add the tomatoes you previously cut in wedges.

Cook for a few minutes more, about 10, then add the olives and stir for a while more. Voilà, the sauce is ready.

Bring the water to boil in a tall, large pot, and tip the pasta in as soon as you see it bubbling. Drain when al dente (about a minute before given cooking time), then pour in the pan with a bit of cooking water. Stir and toss for about a minute, so it's sufficiently sautéed, then serve with a sprinkle of sauce on top.

We can find proof of this composition in many early last century Neapolitan cookbooks, under the name of "aulive e chiappariell", which means "olives and capers", a traditional Campanian dish that we can still find in many local restaurants. Its "vulgar" name ("alla puttanesca" means "done the whore's way") dates back to the turn of the 20th century, where it's said that the owner of a brothel in Naples' Spanish Quarters used to delight his patrons with this very recipe. There are many other tales that offer a different origin to their name, but most of them are about tramps, one way or another.

Spaghetti Aglio e Oglio
(Spaghetti with Oil and Garlic)

Bring a pot of water to boil and tip in the pasta. Sprinkle some oil in a large pan and sauté two crushed garlic cloves, parsley, salt and a chili pepper on low heat. Remove the garlic once it's coloured a little bit, then add a ladle of cooking water and let everything simmer until the pasta is ready.

Once the pasta's done, drain and add it in the saucepan. toss and stir to let it soak in all the different tastes. Serve, with a sprinkle of pecorino cheese if you like.

The so-called "lunchsaver", the poor man's dish par excellence. In the Naples of old, people used to mix in sea pebbles to give it that seafood aftertaste and called it "spaghetti a vongole fujiute" (spaghetti with missing clams). Today, people are using salted anchovies instead, to spice up the taste. It's without a doubt a southern dish, since it's made with olive oil and chili peppers, two ingredients that are always present in our kitchens.

INGREDIENTS

for 4/5 People

- 500 GR SPAGHETTI;
- 2 CLOVES GARLIC;
- 4/5 TBSP. EVO OIL;
- 1 LARGE BUNCH PARSLEY;
- 1 RED HOT CHILI PEPPER;
- SALT TO TASTE.

* * *

Rigatoni al Ragù *(Rigatoni with Ragù)*

Roll the beef chuck slices and the pork rinds, filling them with salt, pepper, diced pecorino cheese, grated garlic and parsley, raisins and pine nuts. Tie everything up, very carefully with a bit of butcher's twine. Roughly chop lard, pancetta and onions. Place into a saucepan with oil and sauté at low heat, until the lard is fully melted and the onion starts frying. Add the rolled steaks, beef chuck, pork rinds and ribs. Cover with a lid and allow them to brown over very low heat, turning them frequently. Searing the meat properly is essential. As soon as the onions start colouring, turn the meat more and more frequently and regularly drizzle with red wine, which will have to evaporate completely. Cook for at least an hour, scraping up to make sure the meat

INGREDIENTS

for 5/6 People

- 500 GR RIGATONI;
- 100 GR SMOKED PANCETTA;
- 1,5 KG FRESH CUT BEEF (TRI-TIP SIRLOIN);
- 1 KG BEEF CHUCK ("FETTE DI LOCENA");
- 500 GR PORK RIBS ("TRACCHIULELLE");
- 200 GR PORK RIND, FOR ROLLS;
- 400 GR SCALLIONS;
- 100 GR LARD;
- 4 TBSP. EVO OIL;
- 300 ML DRY RED WINE;
- 2 KG PEELED SAN MARZANO TOMATOES;
- A SMALL BUNCH OF BASIL;
- SALT TO TASTE.

doesn't stick to the bottom of the pan, then stir continuously.

Turn up the heat, and add the tomatoes you previously turned into sauce. Stir some more to mesh everything together and salt to taste. Cook on low heat for at least a few hours. Take care to regularly scrape the sauce from the bottom of the pan during this time. At the end, add the basil, salt to taste and turn off the heat.

Bring a pot of water to boil. salt, and tip in the pasta, then let it cook for the given time. Drain the pasta, place it in a large bowl, top it with ragù and sprinkle with grated cheese. Serve topped with ragù and small chunks of beef.

This particular recipe is my own way of making ragù, but the same can be said for every other recipe in this book. It's how I prepare it in my own kitchen, the way my mother taught me, even though I changed some things along the way due to a series of different circumstances, mostly dictated by what's available or fresh in the market. Ragù takes a disproportionate amount of time to prepare, which often clashes with our schedule, to the point that our mothers spent the whole morning making it, even though they got up fairly early.

Entire books have been written on this one dish, painstakingly detailing every ingredient with the utmost care and going over every step of the process. Lately, chefs from around the world have been recording videos on how to make Ragù, and each time the recipe gets more complicated and the ingredients more outlandish, way removed from the ragù a normal housewife is used to make. Granted, it's not a simple dish to begin with: the foundation is meat cooked so well, that it almost has to melt in your mouth, and a sauce that's pleasant to the taste.

Talking about Ragù and the Neapolitan heritage, I'm reminded of a poem Eduardo de Filippo dedicated to this dish, which his wife always prepared for him…

despite not being very good at it. De Filippo refers to it as "carne c'a pummarola", or a simple, bland side of meat with tomatoes thrown in.

'O rraù'

« ‹O rraù ca me piace a me
m' 'o ffaceva sulo mammà.
A che m'aggio spusato a te,
ne parlammo pè ne parlà.
Io nun songo difficultuso;
ma luvàmmel' 'a miezo st'uso
Sì, va buono: comme vuò tu.
Mo c' avessem' appiccecà?
Tu che dice? Chest'è rraù?
E io m' 'o mmagno pè m' 'o mangià...
M' 'a faje dicere 'na parola?...
Chesta è carne c' 'a pummarola»

(Only mamma made me
Ragù the way I like it
And since I married you,
we can only talk about it.
I'm not even that picky,
but really, forget all about it.
Okay, alright: have it your way.
What's the use arguing, anyway?
What're you sayin'? This is Ragù?
I'm eating it just because.
Well, can I tell you the truth?
This is just meat and tomato sauce.)

The great Edoardo De Filippo, a notorious playwright in addition to being a poet, never missed the chance to add a reference to ragù in his works, like in the famous comedy "sabato, domenica e lunedì" ("Saturday, Sunday and Monday"), which was made into a film starring Sophia Loren by director Lina Wertmüller.

Risotto alla Pescatora *(Seafood Risotto)*

INGREDIENTS
for 5/6 People

- 500 GR CARNAROLI RICE;
- 250 GR SHRIMP;
- 6 KING PRAWNS;
- 1 CALAMARI;
- 1 CUTTLEFISH;
- 500 GR CLAMS;
- 1 KG MUSSELS;
- 2 CLOVES GARLIC;
- 1 ONION;
- 6 CHERRY TOMATOES ("DATTERINI");
- 2 CUPS WHITE WINE;
- 1 SMALL BUNCH OF PARSLEY;
- CHILI PEPPER AND SALT TO TASTE;
- 4 TBSP. EVO OIL.

Start by preparing the fish fumet: shell the shrimp and prawns, and place the heads and shells in a baking tin, add 3 tomatoes, an onion, a sprinkle of parsley, chili pepper, one liter of salted water and a little white wine; cook for 20 minutes to let the tastes come together, and, once done, filter the resulting broth through a strainer, making sure to squeeze as much liquid as you can.

Place all the seafood in a large saucepan and mix with a bit of parsley and half a cup of water. Drizzle with oil and cook for 5 minutes, until they've all opened up. Drain and set aside the liquid, once again filtering through a strainer. Remove the shell.

Coat a pan in two tbsp. of oil, add a bit of parsley, a little onion and the diced shellfish, then sauté. Pour in about a cup of wine and cook for 20 minutes, then add 2 tomatoes, shrimp and prawns.

Slice the remaining onion and sauté in a pan with crushed garlic and about 2 tbsp. of oil. Once the garlic is a light golden brown, remove it and tip in the rice, which you will cook until nice and toasty. Stir continuously and drizzle with wine, turn up the heat and let it evaporate. Add the fish broth, a little at a time, and cook until it's completely absorbed.

When the rice is almost ready, it's time to mix in the remaining seafood, apart from the prawns which you will set aside, and stir until it's done. Always check if the water level is adequate, and add a knob of butter to make the risotto creamier.

Take it out of the pan, serve garnished with the king prawns you reserved earlier and a sprinkle of minced parsley.

Pasta e Cucozza *(Pumpkin Pasta)*

Peel and dice the pumpkin, then rinse under running tap water. Start frying the garlic in an oil-coated saucepan, then remove when lightly browned, add the diced pumpkin and let it soak in the oil for a few minutes. Then sprinkle with salt, add the diced cherry tomatoes and parsley, sauté for a little while. Afterwards, pour in about 4 cups of water and simmer for 20/25 minutes, until it's become a little creamy. Add some more water, bring to boil and tip in the pasta. Season with salt and chili a few minutes before it's ready. Right before turning off the heat, sprinkle with some grated parmesan and a handful of minced parsley.

Put the lid on the saucepan and wait a few seconds before serving.

INGREDIENTS
for 5/6 People

- 500 GR TUBETTI RIGATI*;
- 800 GR PUMPKIN;
- 3 TBSP. EVO OIL;
- 1 CLOVE GARLIC;
- 5 RED CHERRY TOMATOES;
- CHILI PEPPER AND SALT TO TASTE;
- 50 GR PECORINO CHEESE.

__TUBETTI RIGATI__ are a special type of pasta made in Campania. they resemble small, grooved tubes, and are often used when making Pasta e Cucozza. They should be fairly easy to find, but if there aren't any available at your local market, most types of short pasta will do.

* * *

Pasta e Cavolo *(Cauliflower Pasta)*

Clean the cauliflowers, removing the central stem, rinse under running tap water, then dice. Gently brown the garlic in an oil-coated saucepan, then remove and add the cauliflower. Sauté on medium heat for a few minutes, adding a pinch of salt.

Pour in 4 cups of water and cook for 20/25 minutes until it's a little creamy. Add some water and bring to boil, then tip in the pasta. A few minutes before it's ready, add salt and pepper to taste, along with minced cheese rinds. Right before you turn off the heat, sprinkle with grated pecorino and minced parsley.

Put the lid on the pan and wait a few seconds before serving.

INGREDIENTS
for 5/6 People

- 400/500 GR WHITE CAULIFLOWER;
- 1 CLOVE GARLIC;
- 1 SMALL BUNCH PARSLEY;
- SALT AND PEPPER TO TASTE;
- 50 GR PECORINO CHEESE;
- 500 GR MIXED PASTA;
- 2/3 CHEESE RINDS;
- 3 TBSP. EVO OIL.

Paccheri ai Frutti di Mare *(Seafood Paccheri)*

INGREDIENTS

for 4/5 People

- 500 GR PACCHERI*;
- 500 GR MIXED CLAMS;
- 1 KG MUSSELS;
- 3 TBSP. EVO OIL;
- 1 CLOVE GARLIC;
- 1 SMALL BUNCH PARSLEY;
- 8 RED CHERRY TOMATOES;
- CHILI PEPPER AND
SALT TO TASTE;
- 1 SMALL ONION

Clean the mussels well, cleansing all the impurities from the shell and removing the byssus. Rinse the clams under running tap water.

Place all the seafood in a large saucepan, sprinkle with a bit of parsley and drizzle with oil. Add half a cup of water, then cook for about 5 minutes, until all the clams have opened up. Drain, filter the liquid through a strainer then set aside.

Remove the fruit from the shells, but keep some clams and mussels intact.

Coat a pan in about two tablespoons' worth of oil, then combine a little parsley, onion, garlic (which you will remove as soon as it colours), de-seeded tomato wedges. Sauté for 10 minutes. Add the seafood you shelled previously, along with their water, salt to taste and turn off the heat.

Bring a tall pot of water to boil, add a few pinches of salt, then tip in the paccheri. A minute before given cooking time, drain the pasta and place in a large pan along with the seafood sauce you prepared earlier. Stir, add some parsley, a pinch of chili pepper if you like, and serve with sauce on top, along with the intact mussels and clams you set aside before.

PACCHERI are another Campanian kind of pasta. They look like big, smooth maccheroni. The name literally means "slap(s)".

* * *

Spaghetti del Poverello
(Spaghetti with Egg, Cheese and Pepper)

INGREDIENTS

for 3/4 People

- 300 GR SPAGHETTI;
- 3 FRESH EGGS;
- 2 TBSP. EVO OIL;
- 50 GR GRATED
PECORINO CHEESE;
- SALT AND PEPPER TO TASTE.

Drizzle a little oil in a pan and, when it's hot, gently pour the eggs inside. Cook for just a little while, until the white starts solidifying, adding a pinch of salt. Cook the pasta until very al dente, then drain and tip it in the pan where you cooked the eggs. Season with a pinch of pepper, cheese and salt, stir to combine and the dish is ready.

Spaghetti ai Polpi *(Octopus Spaghetti)*

Carefully clean the octopi, remove the viscera, the mouths and eyes. Sauté in a pan with garlic and oil for a few minutes. Remove the garlic, add the cherry tomatoes, salt to taste and cook for 25/30 minutes with the lid on.

Bring a tall pot of water to boil, then add salt and tip in the spaghetti. A minute before the given cooking time, drain the spaghetti and tip them in the pan with the sauce. Toss and turn the pasta, add parsley and a pinch of chili, if you like. Serve topped with a sprinkle of sauce and a few octopi.

INGREDIENTS
for 4/5 People

- 500 GR SPAGHETTI;
- 1 KG SMALL OCTOPI;
- 2 TBSP. EVO OIL;
- 1 CLOVE GARLIC;
- 1 SPRIG PARSLEY;
- 400 GR CANNED RED CHERRY TOMATOES;
- CHILI PEPPER;
- SALT TO TASTE

* * *

Spaghetti alla Pizzaiola
(Spaghetti with Tomato Sauce and Oregano)

Start by sautéing the garlic in a large pan, remove as soon as it colours. Add the veal slices and sear properly, turning them over a few times. Add the peeled tomatoes and the oregano, along with a pinch of salt. Cook for 20 minutes. Bring a tall pot of water to boil, add a few pinches of salt, then tip in the spaghetti. Drain a few minutes before given cooking time, place in a large pan and pour on the sauce you prepared earlier. Vigorously stir and toss the pasta, and be sure not to overcook it. Season with salt, a pinch of oregano and grated parmesan. Serve with a sprinkle of sauce on top.

INGREDIENTS
for 4/5 People

- 500 GR SPAGHETTI;
- 400 GR VEAL SLICES;
- 600 GR CANNED CHERRY TOMATOES;
- 2 TBSP. EVO OIL;
- 1 CLOVE GARLIC;
- OREGANO AND SALT TO TASTE.

Rigatoni alla Genovese
(Rigatoni Genovese, with Onions and Ground Meat)

INGREDIENTS

for 4/5 People

- 500 gr Rigatoni;
- 400 gr Beef;
- 3 tbsp. EVO Oil;
- 1 kg Onions;
- 2 cups of White Wine;
- 1 Cup of Milk;
- 1 Cup of Warm Water;
- 1 Celery Stalk;
- 2 Carrots;
- Grated Parmesan Cheese;
- Salt and Pepper to taste.

Combine oil, a pinch of salt, minced celery and carrots in a pan, then add the beef, cut in rough pieces, and sauté. Stir around until the meat's fully seared, then deglaze with wine and continue cooking. Once the wine's evaporated a bit, add the onions and pour in about a cup of water. Put a lid on and cook for a few hours. Stir around every once in a while. After a few hours have gone by, pour in milk, letting it simmer in the mixture until it evaporates. After about half an hour turn off the heat, pull out the meat and mince it finely, then place it back in the pan.

Bring a pot of water to boil, tip in the pasta as soon as it reaches boiling point, then drain about a minute before it's fully done. Tip it in a large saucepan together with your sauce. Toss around to let all the tastes come together and add a sprinkle of grated parmesan. Serve topped with a handful of grated parmesan and a pinch of freshly ground pepper.

The origins of this dish are, to this day, unclear: some say it was originally prepared by innkeepers from Genoa that set up shop around Naples' piers, who used to cook meat in this particular way using the leftovers from the day before. The meat itself has to be of at least decent quality, though, to be cooked in almost criminal amounts of onion and usually enjoyed as its own dish. The resulting sauce, however, is always paired with a type of short pasta. Others say that the recipe is the work of an elusive, almost mythical chef called "O' Genovese" (the Genoan), while others yet point to Ippolito Cavalcanti's book of recipes from 1837 as a possible origin, even though nowhere in it is it mentioned a way to make pasta sauce from meat. This dish, in its original incarnation, is surprisingly hard to find today: most people opt for a simpler version of the "Genovese sauce", which is the one I describe in my recipe.

Pasta Fagioli e Cozze
(Pasta with Beans and Mussels)

Leave the beans to soak in a pot with abundant water and a pinch of baking soda, letting them rest for at least a whole night. Then rinse under running tap water and cook them with a laurel leaf for about 40 minutes, turn off the heat and leave them in their own water. Clean the mussels of all impurities and remove the byssus, place in a pan with half a cup of water and cook for about 5 minutes, then stir around to make sure they're all opened up. Turn off the heat, let cool and place in a bowl with their own water, which you will carefully filter with a fine strainer. In a pan, combine garlic, oil, finely minced carrot and celery, tomatoes cut in half, salt and a pinch of chili pepper if you like it spicy. Sauté for about 10 to 15 minutes, take out the garlic, then pour in about 2/3 of the beans whole, blending the remaining part and adding it in soon after. Cook for about 20 minutes, adding a bit of cooking water from the mussels and beans. It's time to cook the pasta in the sauce: add the right amount of water in the pan, which should be about even with the beans, then tip in the pasta. A few minutes before given cooking time, mix in the mussels and salt to taste. Check how much water is left and adjust according to your taste, taking into account it's going to cook for a few more minutes. Once the pasta's done, taste for seasoning, turn off the heat, put the lid on and wait a few seconds before serving.

Pasta and beans tastes great even without mussels. Adding seafood to this simple recipe is a fairly recent idea: most restaurants in Naples today only offer the "beans and mussels" version though, while the original dish can still be found in traditional taverns and trattorias. In my humble opinion, the classic Pasta e Fagioli with cherry tomatoes, pork rind and a sprinkle of cheese rinds remains a delicious, tasteful dish.

INGREDIENTS
for 4/5 People

- 1 KG MUSSELS;
- 500 GR DRIED BEANS;
- 400 GR MIXED PASTA OR DITALONI;
- ½ TBSP. OF BAKING SODA;
- 1 TBSP. EVO OIL;
- 1 GARLIC CLOVE;
- 1 SMALL ONION;
- 1 CARROT;
- 1 CELERY STALK;
- 4/5 RED CHERRY TOMATOES;
- 1 LAUREL LEAF;
- SALT TO TASTE.

"There's no place in the world I love more than my kitchen. It doesn't matter where it is, what it's made of: if it's a kitchen, a place where you cook, I feel great. If possible, I like them practical and lived in. Maybe with a lot of dry, clean cloths, and pearly white tiles. A place I would happily share with the ones I love."

Banana Yoshimoto

Minestra and Soups

"A' cucina piccerella, fa a casa granne"

"A small kitchen makes for a great house"

Neapolitan Proverb

Minestra And Soups

Minestra, which is a kind of watery soup, is perhaps one of the most ancient and traditional Neapolitan foods, to the point that a common slang term for Neapolitans before the 18th century was "mangiafoglie" ("leaf eaters"). Back then pasta wasn't as nearly as widespread it is today, and it was mostly used in the preparation of sweets: only after 1700 did we transition from leaf-chowing to pasta-chowing, since the growing population couldn't really get by on collard greens alone. Traditions are set in stone, though, and a hot legume soup or a vegetables minestra warm the soul and tickle the palate during long, hard winters.

The undisputed Master of Minestra just so happens to be my wife: she jealously keeps all the different recipes on post-it notes strewn all over the house, in nooks and crannies I don't even care to know about, and she's privy to all the tricks to make a tastier soup that her mother (or mine, sometimes) taught her in all these years. She knows all about how to treat the legumes, what's the best meat or fish to use, the cooking time down to the second, all the essentials to make a minestra taste just right. Usually she starts working from the early morning or even the night before, but don't be fooled: she's probably been planning it all week. She's clearly very jealous of her recipes, and she never listens to any advice or explores any variation, especially for the Minestra Maritata, which remains a recipe that's exclusive to a few special days every year, while the others are generally reserved for big gatherings.

- Minestra di Verdure / "Maritata" *(Veggie Minestra)*
- Lenticchie e Scarole *(Lentils and Escaroles Minestra)*
- Fagioli e Scarole *(Beans and Escaroles Minestra)*
- Minestra di verza *(Savoy Minestra)*
- Zuppa di Pesce *(Seafood Stew)*
- Zuppa di Cozze *(Mussel Stew)*

Minestra di Verdure / "Maritata" *(Veggie Minestra)*

INGREDIENTS

for 6/8 people

VEGETABLES

- 1 ESCAROLE;
- 1 SAVOY CABBAGE;
- 3 BUNDLES BROCCOLI;
- 3 BUNDLES CHICORY;
- 3 BUNDLES BEETS (SWISS CHARD);
- 3 TORZELLE*;
- 3 BORAGE;
- 1 CLOVE GARLIC.

FOR THE BROTH:

- 1 KG CHICKEN LEGS;
- 600 GR FAT PORK MEAT;
- 600 GR HEN;
- 2 PORK RIBS;
- 2 PORK RINDS;
- 2 TBSP. EVO OIL;
- 1 WHITE ONION;
- 2 CARROTS;
- 1 CELERY STALK;
- SALT TO TASTE;
- 2 OR 3 CHEESE RINDS, TO GRATE;
- 6 RED CHERRY TOMATOES;
- WATER Q.S.

Let's start by preparing the broth with a minced carrot, onion, celery, tomatoes and all the different meats. Coat a pan in oil (about two tablespoons) and sauté the veggies. As soon as the onion is a light brown, start adding the meat, in order from the thickest to the most tender ones: fat pork, hen, ribs, pork rinds (which you will have previously rolled up and stuffed with garlic and parsley), then the chicken legs at the end. Stir and cook everything well, then add water until the meat is fully submerged. Simmer for a few hours in medium heat, checking to make sure the water level is always above the meat.

Carefully clean the veggies: remove the outermost leaves of the savoy cabbage, then slice it, removing the midrib; pluck the leaves from the broccoli's stalk; cut only the white end from the chicory and beets; take only the leaves from the torzelle and borage. Once the cleaning's done, cook the veggies separately and set aside.

In a large pan, combine garlic, tomatoes and oil and sauté. Take out the garlic after a while and add the veggies you prepared before. Mix in the meat, minced finely and thoroughly cleaned of any bones, along with a little broth to cook, for at least another hour. At the end, add some cheese rinds, salt to taste and serve scorching hot with a sprinkle of grated parmesan and pecorino.

It is through the holy union of vegetables and meat that the Minestra Maritata is born. Some call it the "poor man's relief", made of (sometimes) wild plants and meat leftovers that usually survive the holiday periods. Our grandmas used to say that it cleansed the body after the holiday meals. It's a dish that's easy to prepare despite its complexity: the process itself requires hours for the preparation of the vegetables and cooking of the final mixture. The result is sure to satisfy every customer, though.

---

*TORZELLE are a type of curly-leaved kale. If you can't find any, another kale variant should suffice.

Lenticchie e Scarole *(Lentils and Escaroles)*

Rinse the lentils in running tap water and cook in a water-filled pan, salt to taste and simmer for about 20 minutes. Rinse and clean the escarole, removing the outer leaves, then cut in thin slices and sauté in a pan with a bit of oil and garlic for about 20 minutes. In another saucepan, combine oil, parsley and tomatoes and start sautéing. After a few minutes, add the lentils from before and a sprinkle of chili powder (or crush some dried chili pepper if you have it at home). Once the lentils have soaked in all the flavors, add the other vegetables and cook for about half an hour, pouring in some of the lentils' own cooking water.

At the end, taste for seasoning and add some salt if needed. Serve hot with a sprinkle of pecorino.

INGREDIENTS
for 6/8 People

- 500 GR LENTILS;
- 2 ESCAROLES;
- 6 RED CHERRY TOMATOES;
- 1 CLOVE GARLIC;
- 1 SMALL BUNCH OF PARSLEY;
- 2 TBSP. EVO OIL;
- A PINCH OF CHILI POWDER / CRUSHED CHILI PEPPER;
- SALT TO TASTE.

* * *

Fagioli e Scarole *(Beans and Escaroles Minestra)*

The night before, soak the beans in a bowl filled with water and a binch of baking soda. The following day, rinse the beans and place them in a pot, completely immersed in water. Salt and cook for about an hour.

Rinse and clean the escaroles, removing the outermost leaves, cut in strips and sauté with oil and garlic for about 20 minutes.

In a separate pan, combine oil, garlic, celery and tomatoes and sauté. After a few minutes, add the beans and a pinch of chili powder. When the beans have soaked in the different tastes, add the escaroles and cook for a half hour, pouring in a bit of the beans' cooking water.

When done, taste for seasoning, mix in the cheese rinds, and serve with a dusting of grated pecorino cheese.

INGREDIENTS
for 6/8 People

- 500 GR DRY BORLOTTI BEANS;
- 2 SMOOTH ESCAROLES;
- 6 RED CHERRY TOMATOES;
- 1 CLOVE GARLIC;
- 1 CELERY STALK;
- 2 TBSP. EVO OIL;
- A PINCH OF CHILI POWDER;
- 2 OR 3 CHEESE RINDS, TO BE GRATED;
- SALT TO TASTE.

Minestra di verza *(Savoy Minestra)*

INGREDIENTS
for 3/4 People

- 1 LARGE SAVOY CABBAGE;
- 6 RED CHERRY TOMATOES;
- 1 CLOVE GARLIC;
- 2 TBSP. OIL;
- 1 ONION;
- 250 GR PANCETTA;
- 2 SAUSAGES;
- A PINCH OF CHILI POWDER / CRUSHED CHILI PEPPER;
- SALT TO TASTE.

Clean the savoy, taking out the first few leaves, then cut it in thin slices, removing the midrib. Afterwards, blanch in a large pot for about 20 minutes, then take it out of the water and drain in a colander. Heat some oil in a pan, then add garlic, chopped onion, diced pancetta, the two sausages (after removing the outer skin and slicing in rounds) and a pinch of chili powder or crushed chili pepper. Sauté for about 10 minutes and then tip in the savoy that we blanched earlier. Cook for another 20 minutes, stirring every once in a while. Salt to taste, then serve searing hot with a sprinkle of grated cheese, over (why not?) a tasty bruschetta.

* * *

Zuppa di Pesce *(Seafood Stew)*

INGREDIENTS
for 4/5 People

- 4 RED GURNARDS (ABOUT 400/500 GR);
- 4 REDFISH (ABOUT 400/500 GR);
- 4 WEEVERS (ABOUT 400/500 GR);
- 2 MEDIUM CUTTLEFISH;
- 2 CALAMARI;
- 4 BABY OCTOPUS;
- 8 MEDIUM SHRIMP;
- 12 SLIPPER LOBSTERS ("SPERNOCCHIE");
- 1 KG MUSSELS;
- ½ KG CLAMS;
- 200 GR SEA SNAILS;
- 2 TBSP. EVO OIL;
- 300 GR CHERRY TOMATOES;
- A PINCH OF RED HOT CHILI PEPPER;
- 1 BUNCH BASIL;
- 1 CLOVE GARLIC;
- 1 SMALL ONION;
- 8 SLICES OF STALE BREAD, TO TOAST;
- SALT TO TASTE.

Clean the fish, carefully pulling out all the viscera, then rinse under running tap water and set aside. Clean the seafood from all impurities, remove the mussels' byssus and rinse under running tap water. Remove the entrails, eyes and mouth of the mollusks, cut the calamari and cuttlefish in rounds, then rinse under running tap water. Shell the shrimp, removing the head and the black strand from their backs, and clean the slipper lobsters, trimming the spiky outer shell. rinse the snails in running tap water. Clams and mussels must be cooked separately with a bit of water, after which we pluck them from their shells and filter the cooking water, which we will use later for the stew.

In a large saucepan, mix oil, crushed garlic, minced onion, half of the parsley finely chopped, tomatoes, chili pepper, and sauté for a little while. Pour in some white wine, and as soon as it starts boiling, add the octopus, calamari and cuttlefish, then cook for about 20 minutes, adding a bit of mussel cooking water to bring everything together. After the 20 minutes have gone by, add the shrimp and the snails, and continue cooking for another 10 minutes, always making sure that there's enough liquid in the pan. Season with salt.

In the meantime, toast the sliced bread in the oven, a cast iron skillet or a toaster, then place them on the edge of a soup plate. Pour the stew in with a little sauce, sprinkle with the remaining parsley and add some more chili, if it's to your taste.

* * *

Zuppa di Cozze *(Mussel Stew)*

Clean the mussel shells from all impurities and remove the byssus sticking out of the body. In order to clean thoroughly, place the mussels in a small plastic bag, add a good handful of coarse salt, and shake to rub the salt and shells together. Rinse under running tap water and put in a bowl or colander.

In a large pan with raised edges, combine crushed garlic, half a bunch of parsley, the chili pepper, deseeded tomato wedges and oil. Sauté until slightly soft and tip in the mussels. Put on the lid and simmer. As soon as it starts boiling, the mussels are going to open up. Cook for about 5/6 minutes, stirring a few times, until all the mussel shells are open wide. Sprinkle with the remaining parsley and taste for seasoning, salting a bit if necessary. In the meantime, toast the sliced bread in the oven or a cast iron skillet. When they're ready, place them on the edge of a soup plate, in which you'll serve the mussel stew.

It's customary, in the city of Naples, to make this stew on Holy Thursday. It seems that King Ferdinand I is responsible for this particular custom: wanting to heed the warning of a friar, Gregorio Maria Rocco, who suggested to prepare a simpler, poorer meal to celebrate Easter, he had this dish made only with mussels, specially for the day of Holy Thursday. It will prove to be a huge success among the populace, too.

INGREDIENTS
for 4/5 People

- 2 KG MUSSELS;
- 2 CLOVES GARLIC;
- 8 RED CHERRY TOMATOES;
- 1 SMALL BUNCH PARSLEY;
- ½ RED HOT CHILI PEPPER;
- 200 ML WATER;
- 8 SLICES OF STALE BREAD, TO TOAST;
- 2 TBSP. EVO OIL;
- SALT TO TASTE.

To people who knock at our door we don't ask
'Who's there?'. We say: "Come in and dine with us"

Siberian Proverb

Main Course

"Addò magnano duje ponno magnà pure tre"

Where two can eat, there's probably room for one more.

Neapolitan Proverb

Main Course

Either made of meat or fish, intricately interweaving top-class ingredients or mashing together the simplest stuff, baked in the oven or sautéed in a pan, there are really infinite ways to describe what to cook after the first course of a meal, which is called main course for a good enough reason. Often it's where we derive the sauce for our pasta dishes: a saucy Ragù goes all too well with rigatoni, fish broth is a perfect mate for small pasta and carne alla pizzaiola somehow always finds its way inside a plate of linguine.

- Salsicce e Friarielli *(Friarielli and Sausages)*
- Carne al Ragù *(Meat with Ragù Sauce*
- Baccalà Fritto *(Fried Salt Cod)*
- Fegato con le Cipolle *(Liver with Onions)*
- Polpi alla Luciana *(Octopus with Tomato Sauce)*
- Pesce all'Acqua Pazza *(Boiled Fish with Tomatoes and Parsley)*
- Calamari Ripieni *(Stuffed Calamari)*
- Cozze Gratinate *(Mussels au Gratin)*
- Triglie al Cartoccio *(Red Mullet Baked in Foil)*
- Frittata di Patate *(Potato Omelette)*
- Polpette di Carne *(Meatballs)*
- Polpettone *(Meatloaf)*
- Frittura di Pesce *(Fish Fry)*
- Alici in Tortiera *(Baked Anchovies and Bread Bowl)*
- Parmigiana di Melanzane *(Eggplant Parmesan)*
- Gateau di Patate *(Neapolitan-style Baked Potato Pie)*
- Pizzaiola di Carne *(Meat with Tomatoes and Oregano)*
- Seppie e Patate *(Cuttlefish with Potatoes)*
- Pollo alla Cacciatora
  (Chicken Drumsticks with Vegetables and White Wine)
- Zuppa di Soffritto *(Pork giblets with tomato sauce)*

Salsicce e Friarielli *(Friarielli and Sausages)*

INGREDIENTS

for 4/5 People

- 1,5 KG FRIARIELLI;
- 4 TBSP. OIL;
- 1 CLOVE GARLIC;
- SALT TO TASTE;
- CHILI PEPPER;
- 5 PORK SAUSAGES;
- 1 CUP RED WINE;
- 2 TBSP. OIL.

Clean the friarielli, plucking the leaves from the stalk one by one, then rinse and sauté in a pan, keeping the lid on, for 10/15 minutes. Toss around often to cook uniformly. In the same pan, add minced garlic, oil, a pinch of salt, chili pepper and sauté for another 5 minutes before taking off the heat.

In another pan, cook the sausages whole with a little white wine and oil for about 10 minutes, until they have absorbed some of the liquid. As soon as they're done, place them in the pan with the friarelli and give them a little while, about 10 minutes of cooking, to soak in the taste. Serve hot.

I'm not mincing words when I say that us Neapolitans feel an almost familial love for this dish, or better yet, for this fruit of our earth called "Friariello". We consider it one of our own. It is grown exclusively in Campania, even though we can often find similar products that try to emulate its taste. To that end, there's a funny little ditty that perfectly describes what makes a friariello unique, and it goes like this: "IL friariello nun assumiglia 'a nisciun. Il friariello non parla italiano. Il friariello è autoctono e anarchico: il friariello è napulitano, e tutto questo, la salsiccia, lo sa!" ("The Friariello is unlike any other. The Friariello doesn't speak a word of Italian. The Friariello is a native anarchist: the friariello belongs to Naples, and a good sausage knows it!").

The origins of this local delicacy are pretty well documented, and at the same time they almost feel like a fairytale: it's a story found in the famous "Historia della Vulgata" – a book written by a nameless monk from the Convent of the Crucified and Capuchin Friars in the Decumani area of Naples – and the "Facezie e Minuzie" – another book, this one written by the nuns of a nearby convent.

The story goes that, on a day of february, 1694, there was to be a big celebration in honor of the neighbourhood's "capo". A woman, Donna Immacolata, was well-known in the neighbourhood for making a delicious pizza deep-fried in lard, and she was set to make some just for the occasion. Unfortunately, she noticed too late that she had run out of tomatoes, an essential ingredient in the recipe. Since the guests were about to arrive, Immacolata decided, with a bit of ingenuity, to use the friarielli she kept in the back of her shop, dumping them in the pot of hot, boiling lard. And as if by magic, a wonderful aroma spread from the pot, filling the alley of Sant'Agostino degli Scalzi. Ever since then, friarielli have always been cooked in boiling lard.

* * *

Carne al Ragù *(Meat with Ragù Sauce)*

Start by rolling salt, pepper, diced pecorino, grated garlic and parsley inside the beef chuck slices and pork rinds. Roughly chop the lard, pancetta and onions. Place the resulting mixture in a pan with a bit of oil, and cook at very low heat until the lard melts completely and the onion starts frying. Add the sirloin, the rolled beef chuck and pork rinds, along with the ribs. Cover with a lid and cook, still on very low heat, turning the meat regularly. A good searing is essential. When the onion starts colouring, stir more frequently and regularly sprinkle with wine, which will have to evaporate completely.

Cook for at least an hour more, making sure the meat doesn't stick to the bottom of the pan, and continue stirring. At this point, turn the heat up a bit and add the tomatoes, which you will have turned into sauce beforehand. Salt to taste and stir a little to let the meat bask in all that tomato goodness.

Cook on low heat for a few hours more, and always make sure the sauce doesn't stick to the bottom of the pan.

At the end, garnish with a few fresh basil leaves and salt to taste.

INGREDIENTS
for 5/6 People

- 100 GR SMOKED PANCETTA;
- 1,5 KG FRESH CUT BEEF (TRI-TIP SIRLOIN);
- 1 KG BEEF CHUCK ("FETTE DI LOCENA");
- 500 GR PORK RIBS ("TRACCHIULELLE");
- 200 GR PORK RIND, FOR ROLLS;
- 400 GR SCALLIONS;
- 100 GR LARD;
- 4 TBSP. EVO OIL;
- 300 ML DRY RED WINE;
- 2 KG PEELED SAN MARZANO TOMATOES;
- A SMALL BUNCH OF BASIL;
- ROUGHLY DICED PECORINO CHEESE;
- 50 GR RAISINS;
- 30 GR PINE NUTS;
- SALT TO TASTE.

Baccalà Fritto *(Fried Salt Cod)*

INGREDIENTS

for 4/5 People

- 1 KG SALT COD (NOT TOO THICK);
- FLOUR Q.B.;
- FRYING OIL

Cut the cod in large pieces and leave it to soak for 3 to 4 days in plenty of cold water, which you will replace every 12 hours.

The cod will eventually expand and whiten. Pull it out of the water and drain on a towel. Heat a bit of oil in a pan with raised edges, up to a temperature of about 170°. Flour the salt cod pieces and dip them in oil for about 6/7 minutes (depending on their size), turning to make sure every side is evenly done. Serve hot with a sprinkle of parsley, salt and a drizzle of lemon juice.

Salt cod is, as the name implies, a type of cod that undergoes a salting process to keep it as fresh as possible, without any added chemicals or food processing. It is usually imported from Northern Europe in the fall and winter. there are literally thousands of recipes involving salt cod in Italian cuisine. Neapolitans like to have it fried, and it's been a recurring guest of Christmas dinner for years now. I highly suggest to buy it while still salted, and personally clean it by soaking in water: it's going to take a few days of waiting, but you're not going to regret it. I also suggest buying the fish meat that's closer to the tail, instead of near the belly: it's thinner, which means it's easier to fry and it comes out even crispier.

* * *

Fegato con le Cipolle *(Liver with Onions)*

INGREDIENTS

for 4 people

- 3 MEDIUM WHITE ONIONS;
- 2 TBSP. EVO OIL;
- 500 GR IN 4 CALF'S LIVER SLICES;
- 1 CUP OF WHITE WINE;
- SALT TO TASTE.

Combine oil and roughly sliced onions in a large pan, let colour on low heat until golden. Add the liver, cut in strips, and cook for about 15 minutes. Pour in the white wine and cook for another 15 minutes; the liquid should have dried up by then. Sauté for a little more, salt to taste and serve still hot.

Polpi alla Luciana *(Octopus with Tomato Sauce)*

Carefully clean the octopi, removing the eyes and mouths, then rinse under running tap water. Place in a large enough pan and cook with a little oil, some chili, freshly ground pepper and a bit of crushed garlic. Sauté, add the tomatoes and cook for about 30 minutes. When they're ready, add the olives and parsley. Serve over croutons or use as a pasta topping.

INGREDIENTS

for 4/5 People

- 1,5 KG OCTOPI;
- 600 GR CHERRY TOMATOES;
- 1 CLOVE GARLIC;
- 100 GR BLACK OLIVES;
- A HANDFUL OF CAPERS;
- 1 BUNCH PARSLEY;
- SALT AND PEPPER TO TASTE;
- CHILI PEPPER;
- 3 TBSP. EVO OIL.

* * *

Pesce all'Acqua Pazza
(Boiled Fish with Tomatoes and Parsley)

Clean the fish, removing the gills, the insides and scales. Rinse under running tap water. In a large pan, heat some oil and a garlic clove. Rinse and cut the tomatoes in wedges, then add in the pan and sauté for a few minutes. Mix in half the parsley, chopped, a pinch of salt and the fish, right after. Keep the heat on medium and sprinkle with wine; cook for about 10 minutes, turning the fish at least once. Soon after, add half a cup of water and simmer for a few minutes more. Serve hot, with a sprinkle of chopped parsley, on two slices of toast.

The creation of this dish can be attributed to the fishermen that, on their long days at sea, managed to prepare a meal that was both tasty and nutritious, all with the spare few ingredients they could muster. It seems that even Totò enjoyed it, and often ordered it in the restaurants of Capri, inadvertently endorsing it and setting a lasting trend.

INGREDIENTS

for 5 People

- 4 MEDIUM FISH OF ABOUT 200/250 GR EACH (BASS, SEABREAM, RED SNAPPER);
- 1 CLOVE GARLIC;
- 1 BUNCH PARSLEY;
- 8/10 RED CHERRY TOMATOES ("DATTERINI")
- 1 CUP DRY WHITE WINE;
- SALT AND PEPPER TO TASTE.

Calamari Ripieni *(Stuffed Calamari)*

INGREDIENTS

for 4 People

- 4 MEDIUM CALAMARI;
- 12 RED CHERRY TOMATOES ("DATTERINI");
- 4 TBSP. EVO OIL;
- 1 CLOVE GARLIC;
- 100 GR BLACK OLIVES;
- A HANDFUL OF CAPERS;
- 1 BUNCH PARSLEY;
- BREAD;
- 1 EGG YOLK;
- DRIED BREADCRUMBS Q.S.;
- 1 CUP OF WHITE WINE;
- SALT AND PEPPER TO TASTE.

Clean the calamari, removing the head and tentacles to pull out the viscera sacs, cut out the mouth, eyes and fin from the shell. Rinse and drain. In a bowl, dice 6 cherry tomatoes and add the diced tentacles, chopped parsley, pitted black olives, capers, the bread (cut out the crust, leaving only the white part; soak in water, then squeeze to drain), egg yolk, salt, pepper and a sprinkle of dried breadcrumbs to glue everything together. Stuff the calamari sacs with the resulting mixture, and stitch them close with a bit of butcher's twine. In a pan combine oil, garlic, white wine and calamari, then sauté for a while and add the remaining cherry to-matoes, pour in half a cup of water and cook for about 30 minutes. Don't let the cooking water dry up, and add some if you have to. Serve hot with a sprinkle of cooking water.

* * *

Cozze Gratinate *(Mussels au Gratin)*

INGREDIENTS

for 4/5 People

- 1 KG LARGE MUSSELS;
- 1 CLOVE GARLIC;
- 4 TBSP. OIL;
- 1 SMALL BUNCH BASIL;
- A HANDFUL OF CAPERS;
- STALE BREAD;
- DRIED BREADCRUMBS Q.S.;
- SALT, PEPPER AND CHILI POWDER TO TASTE.

Clean the mussels, scraping all the impurities from the shell with the help of a small knife, and remove the byssus. In order to clean thoroughly, place the mussels in a small plastic bag, add a good handful of coarse salt, and shake to rub the salt and shells together. After 5 minutes, open up the bag and rinse the mussels under running tap water. At this point, force the mussel shell open by placing a small paring knife in between, about where the shell closes off. Try to separate the shell from the meat, and stop when you hit the muscle; cut the muscle off and finish opening up the shell with your bare hands. Remove the meatless side of the shell, drain the liquid inside the mussel in a bowl and place on a platter.

To prepare the filling, mince the garlic and com-bine with parsley, bread white soaked in water and squeezed (almost) dry, chopped capers, a sprinkle of breadcrumbs, salt and pepper, mixing it all together with a drizzle of oil and a bit of liquid from the mussels.

Take a small chunk out of this mixture and place it in the half-shell around the mussels' meat, press lightly to make sure that the shell is "filled". Clean the edges of excess filling and place on a parchment-lined oven tray. Do the same for every other mussel, placing them right next to each other. Sprinkle some dried breadcrumbs over each one and bake in a preheated oven at 170° for 20/25 minutes.

* * *

Triglie al Cartoccio *(Red Mullet Baked in Foil)*

Clean the mullet, removing the gills, the entrails and the scales, then clean them under running water.

Finely mince garlic and parsley, then add the capers and a pinch of salt and pepper. Carve a few sheets of aluminum foil, they'll be your fish wrappers for the evening. Put the mullet dead center in the foil sheet, stuff it with a bit of filling and drizzle with oil, making sure you coat the whole fish. Do the same for the remaining mullet, and remember to coat the outer skin completely, since otherwise they'd stick to the foil. Sprinkle a bit of chopped parsley on top, and wrap up the fish, sticking the extremities of the aluminum foil sheet together diametrically for an easy reopening, and to ensure that no liquid will get out.

Bake in a preheated oven at 180° for about 25 minutes.

INGREDIENTS
for 5/6 People

- 12 MEDIUM RED MULLETS (ABOUT 120/180 GR EACH);
- 2 CLOVES GARLIC;
- 4 TBSP. OIL;
- 1 LARGE BUNCH PARSLEY;
- A HANDFUL OF CAPERS;
- SALT AND PEPPER TO TASTE;
- ALUMINUM FOIL.

Frittata di Patate *(Potato Omelette)*

INGREDIENTS

for 6/7 People

- 800 GR POTATOES;
- 7 EGGS;
- 350 GR STALE BREAD;
- 50 GR GRATED
PECORINO CHEESE;
- 1 BUNCH PARSLEY;
- FRYING OIL;
- SALT AND PEPPER TO TASTE.

Clean and peel the potatoes, then dice and fry in plenty of oil. take them out with a skimmer and finish draining them on a sheet of cooking paper. Slice the bread and then leave it to soak in a bowl of water.

In another large bowl, whisk the eggs, then add salt, cheese, parsley and pepper. Squeeze the soaked bread and add it to the mixture, along with the potatoes. Stir to let all the tastes come together.

Take a pan that's large enough to hold all the mixture you prepared. Heat a bit of oil, making sure the pan's surface is fully coated, then tip in the mixture and cook on low heat for about 15 minutes. Once it starts getting a bit firmer (you can check by moving it around, very carefully), it'll come off the pan's walls. Invert it on a plate or a large flat lid, then place it in the pan again, taking care not to break it apart. Cook for another 15 minutes, always on low heat to avoid overcooking the outside while undercooking the inside. Poke it with a toothpick to check if it's cooked inside. Once again, use a plate or a flat lid to take it out of the pan, then place it on a large platter and wait for it to cool a bit before slicing and serving.

It seems that this dish was brought to Italy by the Spaniards, who called it Tortilla. They also introduced the potato, which was already widely in use in Spain, but unknown to us at the time. Today, we can find Tortillas in almost every café in Spain, even for breakfast. In Naples, this remains a dearly beloved delicacy, stuffed with potatoes or other vegetables, with onions or even "calzone style" with ricotta filling (the so-called "filoscio").

Polpette di Carne *(Meatballs)*

Cut the bread in chunks and soak it in water. Combine meat, eggs, salt, chopped parsley, raisins, pine nuts and pepper in a large bowl, and start mixing together. Soon after, squeeze the bread to drain and add it in the bowl.

Knead for a few minutes, until every ingredient is properly mixed. The mixture should be firm and well put together. In case it isn't, add a sprinkle of breadcrumbs. After mixing, leave for about an hour in the fridge.

In a large saucepan, heat some oil and the whole garlic. After the garlic colours lightly, take it out, and add the tomato puree, basil and salt. Cook for an hour, then take off the heat.

To prepare the meatballs, shape a handful of ground meat into a ball by rolling them in the palms of your hands, applying the slightest bit of pressure. For perfect meatball shape and size, cup the ground meat between your hands: that's about the "correct" measurement. Fill a large saucepan with abundant oil and heat until about 170°. Tip in the meatballs and fry the outside only, as soon as the exterior has browned move them to the boiling, bubbling tomato sauce. Be sure to use a very large pan: every meatball should fit nice and snug, and ideally form a single layer, or two at most. Cook for another half an hour. You can serve immediately, scorching hot, topped with tomato sauce and a sprinkle of grated cheese; or you can bake them in the oven at 180° for about 15 minutes and serve them in terracotta tins with plenty of sauce and a bit of grated cheese.

INGREDIENTS

for 30 Meatballs

- 750 GR GROUND BEEF;
- 250 GR GROUND PORK;
- 250 GR SALT;
- 250 GR STALE BREAD;
- 4 EGGS;
- 1 BUNCH PARSLEY;
- 50 GR RAISINS;
- 20 GR PINE NUTS;
- 50 GR PECORINO CHEESE;
- PEPPER TO TASTE.

FOR THE TOMATO SAUCE

- 1 WHOLE GARLIC;
- 2 TBSP. OIL;
- 1,5 KG TOMATO PUREE;
- 4 BASIL LEAVES;
- SALT TO TASTE.

Polpettone *(Meatloaf)*

INGREDIENTS

for 10 Portions

- 750 GR GROUND BEEF;
- 250 GROUND PORK;
- 20 GR SALT;
- 250 GR STALE BREAD;
- 4 EGGS;
- 1 BUNCH PARSLEY;
- 50 GR RAISINS;
- 20 GR PINE NUTS;
- 50 GR PECORINO CHEESE;
- PEPPER TO TASTE;
- DRIED BREADCRUMBS;
- FOR THE TOMATO SAUCE:
- 1 GARLIC;
- 2 TBSP. OIL;
- 1,5 KG TOMATO PUREE;
- 4 BASIL LEAVES;
- SALT TO TASTE;

FOR THE FILLING

- 2 HARD-BOILED EGGS;
- 100 GR HAM;
- 150 GR SEMI-SWEET CHEESE.

Cut the bread in chunks and soak it in water. Combine meat, eggs, salt, chopped parsley, raisins, pine nuts and pepper in a large bowl, and start mixing together. Soon after, squeeze the bread to drain and add it in the bowl.

Knead for a few minutes, until every ingredient is properly mixed. The mixture should be firm and well put together. In case it isn't, add a sprinkle of breadcrumbs. After mixing, leave for about an hour in the fridge.

In a large saucepan, heat some oil and the whole garlic. After the garlic colours lightly, take it out, and add the tomato puree, basil and salt. Cook for an hour, then take off the heat.

To prepare the meatloaf, place all the ground meat on a sheet of baking paper, and press it into the shape of a square about 1 cm thick. Place the sliced ham, cheese and eggs in the center, and roll the ground meat, closing off the extremities. Wrap everything in the baking paper, fully enveloping the meatloaf, then wrap again in tinfoil. Place in an oven tray and bake in a preheated oven at 200°, for about 30 minutes.

Take the meatloaf out of the oven, unwrap it and gently place it in a large enough round pan. Pour the sauce in and cook for another 30 minutes, making sure that it doesn't stick to the bottom of the pan.

When it's ready, serve it sliced with its sauce and a sprinkle of grated cheese on top.

Frittura di Pesce *(Fish Fry)*

Clean the calamari, removing the head and tentacles to take out to the viscera sacs inside, cut out the mouths, the eyes and the fins from the shell, then cut the shell in rounds, rinse and drain.

Clean the fish, removing the gills and taking out the entrails, but keeping the scales. Rinse the shrimp.

Place all the seafood on a cloth to drain.

Liberally flour all the fish and, using a large enough strainer, drain all the excess flour. Heat up a bit of oil in a large pan, bring it to 170° and start frying. Make sure that the oil keeps the same temperature throughout, so that the flour doesn't stain it too much. If that's the case, then it's time for a pit stop and an oil change.

Fry the fish first (which will cook for 5/6 minutes, and will have to be flipped at least once), then the calamari (which need to fry a few minutes more than the fish) and the shrimp (which only need to stay in two or three minutes tops).

As soon as they're ready, take the fish out with a skimmer and drain on cooking paper. Once everything's good and done, serve in mixed fish/shellfish portions with a sprinkle of parsley and some lemon wedges to squeeze.

INGREDIENTS
for 4/5 People

- 2 CALAMARI;
- 5 SMALL CODS (60/70 GR EACH)
- 5 MEDIUM RED MULLETS (80/100 GR EACH);
- 10 LARGE ANCHOVIES;
- 500 GR SMALL SHRIMP;
- FLOUR Q.S.;
- SALT TO TASTE;
- 2 LEMONS;
- 1 BUNCH PARSLEY;
- FRYING OIL.

* * *

Alici in Tortiera *(Baked Anchovies and Bread Bowl)*

Clean and wash the anchovies, remove the head and entrails, open them up and take out the spine. Rinse under running tap water. Drizzle some oil in a baking tin and spread the anchovies in a sunburst pattern. Top with some more oil, minced garlic, parsley, a pinch of oregano and salt. Cook for about 5 minutes, during which you'll pour in about half a cup of water with some drops of lemon juice.

INGREDIENTS
for 2/3 People

- 400 GR MEDIUM ANCHOVIES;
- 3 TBSP. EVO OIL;
- 1 CLOVE GARLIC;
- 1 BUNCH PARSLEY;
- LEMON JUICE (ABOUT HALF A LEMON'S WORTH);
- OREGANO AND SALT TO TASTE.

Parmigiana di Melanzane *(Eggplant Parmesan)*

INGREDIENTS

for 8/10 Portions

- 2 KG EGGPLANTS;
- FRYING OIL;
- 5 EGGS;
- FLOUR AND DRIED BREADCRUMBS Q.S.;
- 100 GR GRATED PARMESAN CHEESE;
- 500 GR MOZZARELLA "FIOR DI LATTE";
- 1 SMALL BUNCH BASIL;
- 200 GR HAM;
- SALT TO TASTE;

FOR THE TOMATO SAUCE

- 1 WHOLE GARLIC;
- 2 TBSP. OIL;
- 2 LT. TOMATO PUREE;
- 4 BASIL LEAVES;
- SALT TO TASTE.

Wash and peel the eggplants, then slice and place in a colander, alternating eggplant slices and salt. Place a large plate on top and add a bit of weight over it: the pressure will drain the excess vegetable water. After a few hours, rinse thoroughly and drain on a cloth. Prepare three plates or small bowls, one with flour, one with dried breadcrumbs and one with whisked eggs, salt and grated parmesan cheese. Dip the eggplants in flour, then in the egg mixture, then finally in the dried breadcrumbs. Heat some oil in a pan, until it reaches about 170°, and then start frying. Once they're nice and crispy, take them out of the pan and drain on a plate covered in cooking paper.

In a large saucepan, heat oil and garlic, until the garlic is lightly coloured. Take it out and add the tomato sauce, parsley and salt. Cook for an hour and then turn off the heat.

Now, it's time to start putting your parmesan together. Coat the bottom of a casserole dish in tomato sauce, and layer eggplants on top. Continue alternating between eggplants, sauce and the other ingredients: diced mozzarella, ham, grated cheese, parsley and a pinch of salt. Do this until you run out of ingredients.

Top with a last layer of sauce, a sprinkle of parsley and a few basil leaves. Cook in a preheated oven at 180° for about an hour. Let it sit for a bit before serving.

Once again, "The Gentleman's Cookbook" by Vincenzo Corrado was the first to describe a similar dish, originally made with zucchini, but eventually with other added ingredients. Eggplant parmesan is still widely popular in Naples, even though many restaurants and rotisseries have developed a lighter version of the recipe.

Gateau di Patate *(Neapolitan-style Baked Potato Pie)*

Clean and blanch the potatoes, boiling them whole and unpeeled in hot water for 35/40 minutes. Let them cool, peel and mash them with a potato masher. When they've cooled down a bit, combine with eggs, diced butter, salt, pepper, chopped parsley, diced provola and salame. Mix everything together and salt to taste.

Butter up a large baking tin and sprinkle with dried breadcrumbs. Place the potato mixture on top and use a fork to press and spread it all over the tin. Dust the surface with breadcrumbs.

Bake in a preheated oven at 180° for 40 minutes, until a thin golden crust has formed on top. Let it sit for a while, but serve warm.

Tradition states that this dish was prepared for the first time in 1768, for the wedding between archduchess Marie Caroline and Ferdinand IV Bourbon. It was a known fact that the future Queen didn't particularly like Neapolitan food, so she hired a team of French chefs for the royal ceremony. It was these very French chefs who offered the guests a new dish, prepared especially for the occasion: a small, savoury potato pie. The "Gattò" is, for all intents and purposes, a Neapolitan dish, prepared with the typical ingredients of Campanian cuisine. The name "Gattò" derives from the French word "Gateau", which denotes every type of sweet or salty pie, phonetically adapted for the Neapolitan dialect. In and around Naples, the term "Gattò" is used exclusively to refer to the salty potato pie, as opposed to the more generic "Gateau". Today, "Gattò di patate" is a household name in Italian gastronomy.

INGREDIENTS
for 8/10 People

- 2 KG POTATOES;
- 500 GR PROVOLA;
- 200 GR DICED MORTADELLA;
- 100 GR DICED SALAME NAPOLI;
- 100 GR BUTTER;
- 100 GR PECORINO CHEESE;
- 4 EGGS;
- 1 BUNCH PARSLEY;
- SALT AND PEPPER TO TASTE;
- DRIED BREADCRUMBS Q.B.

Pizzaiola di Carne *(Meat with Tomatoes and Oregano)*

INGREDIENTS

for 5/6 People

- 600 GR VEAL SLICES;
- 600 GR CANNED CHERRY TOMATOES;
- 2 TBSP. EVO OIL;
- 1 CLOVE GARLIC;
- OREGANO AND SALT TO TASTE.

Heat the oil in a large saucepan. Take it out as soon as it colours, and add the meat, which you will sear, turning it a few times. Add the peeled tomatoes oregano and a pinch of salt. Cook for about 30 minutes.

* * *

Seppie e Patate *(Cuttlefish with Potatoes)*

INGREDIENTS

for 4/5 People

- 500 GR SMALL CUTTLEFISH;
- 500 GR POTATOES;
- 4 TBSP. EVO OIL;
- 1 GARLIC CLOVE;
- 1 MEDIUM ONION;
- 1 CUP DRY WHITE WINE;
- 1 BUNCH PARSLEY;
- 100 GR BLACK OLIVES;
- A HANDFUL OF CAPERS;
- SALT AND PEPPER TO TASTE.

Clean the cuttlefish, removing the head and tentacles, taking out the viscera and the bone from the shell, then rinse thoroughly under running water and drain. In a large pan, fry the garlic in oil, take out when lightly coloured. Add minced onion, parsley, then tip in the calamari and sauté. After about 7/8 minutes, pour in the wine and cook for another 10 minutes. Then add the potatoes, olives, capers and a cup of water. Simmer for 30 minutes still, making sure that there's enough liquid in the pan.

* * *

Pollo alla Cacciatora
(Chicken Drumsticks with Vegetables and White Wine)

INGREDIENTS

for 4/5 People

- 10 CHICKEN DRUMSTICKS;
- 5 EGGS;
- 50 GR PARMESAN CHEESE;
- FLOUR AND DRIED BREADCRUMBS Q.S.
- CURRY, SALT AND PEPPER TO TASTE;
- FRYING OIL;
- 3 CANS, 400 GR EACH SAN MARZANO TOMATOES;
- 3 TBSP. EVO OIL;
- 1 MEDIUM ONION;

Clean and skin the chicken drumsticks, then dry on a clothes for a few minutes. Cover them in flour, then dip them in a mixture of whisked eggs, grated cheese, salt and pepper. Finally, dust with a mix of dried breadcrumbs, spices and salt. Fry them a little in boiling oil, just the time to turn the breading a light golden brown, then take them out of the oil and drain on cooking paper.

In an oven tray with raised edges, heat some oil, then add chopped onions and garlic, tomatoes and plenty of chili. Add a cup of white wine and cook for about 10 minutes.

Afterwards, add olives and the chicken drumsticks. Seal the tray with some tinfoil, place in a preheated oven at 200° and cook for about 40 minutes. Serve hot, fresh out of the oven.

- 1 GARLIC CLOVE;
- 1 CUP DRY WHITE WINE;
- 200 GR PITTED BLACK OLIVES;
- CHILI PEPPER Q.B.

* * *

Zuppa di Soffritto (Pork giblets with tomato sauce)

The day before, cut all the giblets into smallish chunks and let them sit in a large bowl filled with water, it'll help drain the excess blood.

The following day, brown the garlic in about ½ of the lard. Take the garlic out and tip in the giblets, which you will have drained in the meantime, and sauté until they let out a fair amount of liquid. Take them out of the pan and reserve the liquid for later.

Sauté the chopped onion and laurel leaves in the other half of the lard. Tip in the giblets again, and, after a bit of sautéing, pour in the wine. Cook for another 20 minutes, then add the pepper paste, both sweet and spicy, and cook for about an hour on low heat. Add the giblets' water, which you set aside earlier, to dilute if necessary.

Serve scalding hot with a side of bruschetta, or use as a spaghetti or bucatini sauce, with a dusting of grated cheese.

INGREDIENTS
for 4/5 People

- 1 KG PORK GIBLETS (LUNGS, HEART, SPLEEN, WINDPIPE, LIVER)
- 1 LARGE ONION;
- 2 CLOVES GARLIC;
- 4 LAUREL LEAVES;
- 300 GR LARD;
- 200 ML DRY RED WINE;
- SWEET AND SPICY PEPPERS PASTE;
- SALT AND CHILI PEPPER TO TASTE.

"Napule è nu paese curioso: è nu teatro antico, sempre apierto. Ce nasce gente ca senza cuncierto scenne p''e strate e sape recità"

Naples is a wonderland: it's an old theatre that's never been closed. People are born there who, with no rhyme or reason, take to the streets and know how to act.

Eduardo de Filippo

Desserts

"Solitude is for the spirit what food is for the body"

Lucius Annaeus Seneca

Desserts

This topic is especially dear to me. I consider desserts to be my one true passion, and I've been baking since I was only a little boy. I believe that our territory holds an almost unlimited potential when it comes to the sheer variety of desserts in our culinary portfolio. Many of them aren't really part of our "local tradition": instead, they were imported here, since our land has always been a crossroads of different cultures and personalities, and many times our people has all too readily made a foreign recipe its own.

The concept of dessert goes beyond the simple idea of food, at least for someone from the austral side of Italy. It's not uncommon, when you visit friends or family, to bring a tray of desserts with you as a present. This works for every occasion, and if you really want to impress, you can bake your own to give.

A dessert brings people together, it's an augury of well-being for the future. And for those of us who prepare them, a dessert is a way to feel good, and I assure you that it does.

In general, the art of cooking, if pursued with passion, helps us think and reflect on ourselves. To shape different ingredients into a good dessert, though, one must possess great patience and focus: in the end, however, you're rewarded with a wonderful feeling in seeing others enjoying your handiwork.

- Pasta Graffe *(Fried Krapfen Dough)*
- Pastiera di Grano *(Cooked Wheat Easter Cake)*
- Babbà *(Yeasted Rhum Cake)*
- Torta Caprese *(Almond and Chocolate Flourless Cake)*
- Chiacchiere *(Carnival Fritters)*
- Zeppole di San Giuseppe *(Fried Dough Balls with Powdered Sugar)*
- Migliaccio *(Lemon Ricotta Cake)*
- Zeppole di Assunta con le Patate *(Fried Dough with added Potatoes)*
- Pastiera di Pasta *(Pasta Cake)*
- Delizia al Limone *(Lemon Delight)*
- Sfogliatelle Frolle *(Pastry filled with Choux)*
- Sfogliatelle Ricce *(Clam-shaped Puff Pastry)*
- Deliziose *(Custard and Hazelnut Filled Short Pastry Cookies)*
- Struffoli *(Honey Balls)*
- Crostata di Frutta Fresca *(Fresh Fruit Tart)*
- Torta Ricotta e Pera *(Pear Ricotta Cake)*
- Fiocchi di Neve (Snowflakes) *(Cream-filled Fluffy Pastries)*
- Panettone Prestofatto *(Readymade Panettone)*

Pasta Graffe *(Fried Krapfen Dough)*

INGREDIENTS

for about 20 Graffe

- 500 GR TYPE 00 FLOUR;
- 500 GR MANITOBA FLOUR;
- 10 GR SALT;
- 30 GR SUGAR;
- ABOUT 500 ML WATER OR MILK;
- 25 GR BREWER'S YEAST;
- 100 GR BUTTER;
- 2 EGGS;
- 1 GRATED LEMON ZEST;
- A PINCH OF CINNAMON.

Melt brewer's yeast and sugar in warm water or milk, then soften up the butter by keeping it over the cup. Spread an even layer of sifted flour on a flat surface, where you'll start adding the ingredients one by one (eggs, butter, etc.) and knead until a soft, chewy dough is formed. Note that it shouldn't stick to the hands when you grab it.

Let it sit in a bowl, covered with some film so it doesn't dry up, until it has doubled in size. Length of time varies based on ambient temperature.

You can give different shapes to the resulting dough: the classic "donuts", for which you first make a stick (it can be however long you want) and then join the extremities in a circular shape; bites, which are small buns flat on top; and "cannoli", formed by coiling a stick of dough around a lightly buttered cannoli mold.

Whichever style you choose, let the shaped dough grow for a while, but not too much. Start frying in a pot of hot oil, with the heat on medium high. Don't go overboard on the temperature, since it's possible to overcook the outside and undercook the inside.

Stir and turn during cooking and, once they're sufficiently brown, take them out and drain the excess oil on a sheet of cooking paper.

Fill a separate, tall bowl with sugar, vanilla extract and a bit of cinnamon. Dip the treats in until completely covered in sugar.

For the "cannoli", remove the mold right after browning, and fill with cream or custard.

This little treat, too, seems to have its origins in the faraway, whimsical land of Germany, where they're still called Krapfen. It was brought to Naples by the Austrians in 1700., although there are countless different instances of a similar pastry in the rest of Italy, with only slight variations in the ingredients. In our city, it's custom to prepare a similar dough for St. Joseph's Day, only adding a few blanched potatoes to the mix.

Pastiera di Grano *(Cooked Wheat Easter Cake)*

FOR THE SHORT PASTRY:

Combine all the ingredients by hand or with a stand mixer planetary, add the eggs and the softened butter, mix everything as quickly as you can. Wrap the resulting dough in cling film and let it sit in the fridge for a few hours.

FOR THE CREAM:

Drain the Grano Cotto of its water, then place it in a stockpot along with milk, a knob of butter, a little grated orange and lemon zest. Heat it all up and stir until the milk is completely absorbed. Drain the cream in a strainer, removing the excess liquid. In another large bowl, mix ricotta with sugar and add the eggs, whisked beforehand, grated lemon and orange zest, crushed clove (don't forget to remove the stem), grated or diced citron. Now, add all the different aromas to the mixture, along with the cold wheat cream you prepared before and, if you want the end result to taste a little more delicate, a bit of custard.

Take the short pastry out of the fridge and roll it out in an even layer, about 4/5 mm thick. Butter a 30 cm round cake tin with margarine, then carefully line it with dough, making sure it sticks firmly. Fill with cream, making sure to leave about a centimeter free, counting from the edge. Cut the remaining pastry in strips and use them to decorate the pastiera, placing them diagonally on top of the cake, going in different directions to create lozenge shapes.

Bake in a preheated oven at 170° for about an hour, until the cake becomes light brown. You can puncture with a toothpick to check if the cream inside is cooked or not.

Once sufficiently cooled, dust with powdered sugar before serving.

INGREDIENTS

For a 30 cm wide, 5 cm tall Mold

FOR THE SHORT PASTRY

- 500 GR TYPE 00 FLOUR;
- 250 GR BUTTER;
- 250 GR SUGAR;
- 2 WHOLE EGGS;
- GRATED ½ ORANGE ZEST;
- GRATED ½ LEMON ZEST;
- 2 SACHETS VANILLIN;
- A PINCH OF BAKING SODA;

FOR THE FILLING

- 1 JAR GRANO COTTO (COOKED WHEAT, ABOUT 500/600 GR);
- 300 GR MILK;
- 1 SACHET VANILLIN OR ½ TSP. VANILLA EXTRACT;
- 500 GR FRESH RICOTTA;
- 400 GR SUGAR;
- 5 WHOLE EGGS;
- 1 GRATED LEMON ZEST;
- 1 GRATED ORANGE ZEST;
- 2 VIALS WILDFLOWER EXTRACT;
- 1 VIAL ORANGE BLOSSOM WATER;
- 200 GR CANDIED CITRON AND ORANGE;
- A PINCH OF CINNAMON;
- 3 CLOVE.

Pastiera must always be prepared the day before serving, since the ricotta and all the different essences ideally need a few hours to mesh together in a delicious and coherent whole.

When you think about "Neapolitan desserts", the mind inevitably wanders to the Pastiera and Babbà. In my travels around the world, and my occasional visits to Italian restaurants abroad, I could correctly guess the background of a chef just by the presence of this dessert in the menu. For our people, Pastiera used to be an Easter cake. Today, though, bakeries have a slice ready to enjoy every time of the year, and you can even find it in cafés next to a good cup of coffee.

It seems that the famous Pastiera owes its creation to a crafty nun in the convent of San Gregorio Armeno, around the 16th century. The convent's residents were veritable masters in the art of the Pastiera, which became a symbol of Christianity with its simple ingredients like wheat, eggs, ricotta and spices imported from all over the world. During Easter time, many were gifted to noble families, who appreciated them all too much. It's said that even the usually stoic Queen Marie Therese of Spain, second wife of notorious glutton "King Bomb" Ferdinand II Bourbon and herself the "Queen Who Never Smiles", actually let slip a small chuckle when she tasted the beloved Pastiera.

"Making my wife smile is something only a Pastiera can do: now I'll have to wait until next Easter to see her smile again", said King Ferdinand.

Babbà *(Yeasted Rhum Cake)*

As with every other kind of leavened dough, the making of a good Babbà has a fundamental premise: the leavening times inevitably vary based on the temperature of our "cooking habitat". Ideally, you'll want a mild, stable, warm-ish temperature. It's very important not to rush and check the growth of the dough quite often, no matter how much time it takes.

FOR THE PRE-DOUGH:

Melt the yeast in warm water, with a teaspoon of sugar to favor the leavening process, then whisk together all the ingredients in a bowl. You'll get a soft, mushy dough, which you will leave to rest in a warm spot, covered with a cloth.

With the right temperature, it should double in size in about half an hour.

FOR THE DOUGH:

Combine the pre-dough, flour, sugar and eggs in a stand mixer's bowl and let it run until you get a uniform mixture. At this point add butter a little at a time, along with a pinch of salt. The dough will be a little flabby at first, so continue mixing until it becomes elastic and comes off the sides of the bowl. That should take about half an hour with a stand mixer. The dough will be ready when it looks "shiny" and has a firm, while still soft, texture.

It has to be so elastic that a single stick can be stretched a few centimeters without breaking.

Cover the dough with a cloth, and let sit until it doubles in size.

This process, done by hand, requires a lot of time and stamina: the desired result, a soft dough filled with air, is mostly dependent on a prolonged effort, which tends to be really draining.

The dough has to be tightly sealed to prevent

INGREDIENTS
for a 28/30 cm Babbà

FOR THE PRE-DOUGH

- 50 GR MANITOBA FLOUR;
- 50 GR WARM WATER;
- 12,5 GR BREWER'S YEAST;
- 1 TSP. SUGAR;

FOR THE DOUGH

- 250 GR MANITOBA FLOUR;
- 2 WHOLE EGGS;
- 4 EGG YOLKS;
- 30 GR SUGAR;
- 100 GR BUTTER;
- A PINCH OF SALT
- FOR THE SYRUP ("BAGNA"):
- 1 LT WATER;
- 700 GR SUGAR;
- 2 LEMONS' ZEST;
- 250 GR RHUM;
- 50 GR APRICOT JELLY.

the dough's surface to come into contact with air. I suggest using cling film and leaving a little space on the sides to avoid stunting the dough's growth.

As soon as it grows to double its size, it's time to get your hands dirty. Literally. Butter up your palms and place the dough in an equally buttered babbà mould, trying to spread it evenly, covering about a third of the mould. Naturally, the dough is going to lose some of its size, so let it grow in a warm place until it reaches the top of the mould (and even beyond!). Be careful not to let it spill over, though.

Cooking: the oven has to be pre-heated at 180°, otherwise it's going to mess up our recipe. Cook for about 20 minutes.

Take the Babbà out of the oven and check to see if it's a browned. In case it's still a bit moist, put it back in the oven for a few more minutes. If you followed every step perfectly, then our babbà will be a nice golden brown, light and uniform. Wait for it to cool a bit before removing it from the mould, and let it cool completely on a wire rack. You can only add the syrup when it's cold.

ON THE TOPIC OF SYRUP:

Boil the water with sugar and lemon zest for 10 minutes, making sure not to cut the "lemon white" as it gets bitter when cooked. Cool, then remove the lemon zest and add rhum.

Place the babbà in a tall container, large enough to sit in comfortably, leaving a bit of working space for your hands. Pour the syrup on top, scraping the liquid that falls on the bottom and putting it on top again, until the babbà is completely soaked. Carefully grab it with your hands and move it in a round platter, melt the jelly and brush it over the entire surface, so as to delay drying. The babbà, like many other syrupy desserts, has to be eaten right after soaking, which means in the same day. You can enjoy it later, too, if you repeat the soaking process, since it's naturally going to dry and become stale.

It's also possible, with a bit of care, to prepare everything and then only soak the babbà when you intend to eat it.

Serving with custard and fresh fruit could be a good idea to enrich the taste and presentation.

With the same process you can also prepare single-portion babbà, using specific moulds filled to about 3/4ths of their height, to ensure that the dough doesn't spill over after growing.

The loving tenderness that Neapolitans feel for this dessert can only be explained in the context of "Napoletanità", of "being neapolitan", our dasein, our raison d'etre. As with every such concept, it can't be easily put into words, especially if you've never lived, not even for a day, in Naples. Its very name, and how it's pronounced, is inextricably linked to the sound of our dialect. "Babbà", written with two "b"s and pronounced with one, has a special meaning for Neapolitans. Telling someone that they're a "babbà" means (with nary a trace of irony!) that they're a wonderful human being with a brilliant mind, while saying "just like a babbà" means that something's turned out well. We owe its origin, like with many other dishes and desserts in Neapolitan cuisine, to the relationship that the great metropolis entertained with the European nobility: a similar dessert was originally imported from abroad and over time became what we know today as the Babbà.

We can trace its true origins, though, to the Polish King Stanislaw Leszczynski, father-in-law to Louis XV of France; Leszczynski used to dabble in culinary experimentation and, being completely toothless, couldn't enjoy desserts like the Alsatian gugelhupf, that he found too dry for his tastes. He decided, then, to soften it up by soaking it in Tokay and syrup.

Torta Caprese *(Almond and Chocolate Flourless Cake)*

INGREDIENTS

For a cake about 26 cm wide

- 300 GR ROUGHLY CHOPPED ALMONDS;
- 60 GR ROUGHLY CHOPPED HAZELNUTS;
- 250 GR DARK CHOCOLATE, AT LEAST 70% CACAO;
- 250 GR SOFT BUTTER;
- 250 GR SUGAR;
- 6 EGGS;
- GRATED LEMON ZEST;
- TIP OF A TEASPOON OF VANILLA EXTRACT;
- 1 TBSP. RHUM;
- POWDERED SUGAR.

Mince the chocolate into chips and melt in a pot or microwave oven, then cool. Separate the yolks from the egg white, making sure the eggs are at ambient temperature, otherwise they may not turn out the way we want to. Whisk the butter together with half the sugar and tip in the yolks one at a time. Continue whisking, then add in the dark chocolate and the roughly chopped almonds and hazelnuts, mixing everything together well.

Whip up the egg whites with the remaining sugar and a pinch of salt, until you get a thick, firm cream. What comes next is a very delicate procedure: combining the whipped egg whites together with the yolk mixture. Use a spatula and scoop up the whites from the bottom, gently folding them into the chocolate batter, taking care not to deflate it.

Pour the mixture a well-buttered baking tin, as the caprese batter tends to stick to the tin during cooking. If you're just starting out, or if it's your first time making a cake like this one, I suggest using baking paper, sticking it to the tin with a few small knobs of butter or margarine.

Bake in a preheated oven at 170° for at least 60 minutes, and make sure the temperature never rises past that. The cake is full of butter and eggs, and higher temperatures tend to crust the outside of the cake while leaving the inside raw.

Take it out of the oven, let it sit a while, then place it on a wire rack to cool completely. Dust with powdered sugar before serving.

Chocolate desserts always elicit a pleasure response in the customer, and this cake in particular feels moist and soft to the palate, due to it being completely flourless. This characteristic is closely tied to tis origin, at least according to the people of Capri, the isle where it was created. It's told that a talented chef called Carmine Fiore, in the process of making lunch for a group of mobsters with ties to Al Capone's circle, forgot to add the flour to a cake he was baking. The result was a dessert that was moister than usual, while still being incredibly delicious. However, it's more likely that the Caprese owes its success to Totò, who enjoyed it often on his trips to Capri.

* * *

Chiacchiere *(Carnival Fritters)*

Combine all the dry ingredients on a pastry board, then add the softened butter, the eggs, the shot of liquor and a pinch of salt.

Mix everything together until you get a soft, yet firm dough. Roll this dough into a ball, wrap it in cling film and store in the fridge for about an hour.

After the hour's passed, lightly flour the pastry board, take a bit of dough and roll it out in a thin layer with a rolling pin. Then, using a pasta wheel, cut it into strips of varied lengths, which you will later fold in different spots when frying.

Fill a non-stick frying pan with plenty of oil and heat until about 170°. To check if the oil's reached the right temperature (in case you don't have a kitchen thermometer at home), just place a small piece of dough in the pan: if it starts sizzling, then you can start frying.

As soon as the Chiacchiere get crispy and brown, take them out with a skimmer to drain the excess oil and place them on a sheet of cooking paper.

Serve on a platter with a sprinkle of powdered sugar on top. Chocolate cream, marmalade or sweet dessert wine go quite well with a plate of Chiacchiere.

In the Romans' time it seems that Chiacchiere were literally mass-produced to serve the commoners during Saturnalia (the equivalent of our Mardi Gras). Neapolitan folklore states that the name Chiacchiere (which means "chatter") derives from Queen Margherita of Savoy, who had them prepared to lighten up the conversations with her guests. Chiacchiere can be found all over Italy today, with slight variations on the name and ingredients.

INGREDIENTS

- 400 GR FLOUR;
- 60 GR BUTTER;
- 2 WHOLE EGGS;
- 25 GR SUGAR;
- ½ TSP. BAKING SODA;
- 1 SHOT GLASS LIQUOR (STREGA, MARSALA, ANISEED);
- A PINCH OF SALT;
- POWDERED SUGAR;
- FRYING OIL.

Zeppole di San Giuseppe
(Fried Dough Balls with Powdered Sugar)

INGREDIENTS

for 30 Zeppole

- 250 ML WATER;
- 10 GR SALT;
- 100 GR BUTTER;
- 230 GR TYPE 00 FLOUR;
- 5 LARGE EGGS;
- FRYING OIL;

FOR THE CUSTARD

- 15 GR TYPE 00 FLOUR;
- 15 GR CORN STARCH;
- 250 GR MILK;
- 1 LEMON ZEST;
- 60 GR SUGAR;
- 2 EGG YOLKS;
- VANILLA EXTRACT;
- FOR THE GARNISH:
- TINNED SOUR CHERRIES;
- POWDERED SUGAR.

Start by preparing the custard. In a large pan, whisk the egg yolks and sugar, then add the flour and cornstarch. Boil the milk separately with some lemon zest and vanilla extract, then add to the egg mixture a little at a time (don't forget to remove the lemon zest first). Whisk everything together and heat it up, cooking for 3 or 4 minutes, then turn the heat off but keep on stirring. To avoid developing a surface film, dust with a layer of sugar or cover the surface with some cling film.

It's time for the paté à choux. Fill a pot with water, add a pinch of salt, butter and bring to heat. Turn off the heat as soon as the butter's melted and the water's boiling, then pour in the flour, all at once, and whisk together with a ladle until you get a uniform dough.

Put the pot back on low heat and stir until a whitish layer forms on the bottom of the pot. Take it out of the fire once again and wait until cool.

Add the eggs to the dough, one at a time, putting one in only when the previous one is fully absorbed.

Heat up plenty of oil in two pans: the first will have to be at about 120°, gently sizzling, to allow you to turn the zeppole around so that they can grow uniformly. When they've grown to size, grab a skimmer and move them to the other pan with oil at 170°. Cook them inside the sizzling oil, turning a few times, until completely brown.

"Donut" Zeppole: Cut some baking paper into 10x10 squares. Put the mixture inside a star-tipped piping bag and draw a circle on the paper squares. Dip the zeppole, paper and all, in the oil. The paper will come off after a few seconds, so pluck it out with tweezers. Go through the same process as above, frying in two pans, then take them out and place them on a sheet of cooking paper.

Let the zeppole cool, then, with the help of a piping bag, fill the zeppole with custard and 1 or 2 sour cherries. Dust with powdered sugar and serve.

If you want to bake them in the oven, instead, you'll have to add about 50 grams of butter to the dough.

Once again use a star-tipped piping bag to form donuts, directly on an oven tray (which you will have lined in baking paper). Don't forget to leave some room in between to grow.

Bake at 220° for 15/20 minutes and then for an additional 10 minutes at 180°, until they've nicely grown into a crispy golden brown.

Turn off the oven and wait for a few minutes before taking them out. The paté à choux is very sensitive to temperature: it needs a lot of heat to grow, then it has to cook for a while in that same heat before drying at a lower temperature.

* * *

Migliaccio *(Lemon Ricotta Cake)*

Bring a pot of water and milk to boil, with butter and a pinch of salt. Gently pour in the semolina and cook for about 10 minutes, until it comes off the sides. In another bowl, mix the ricotta with sugar, extracts, lemon and orange zest and eggs.

As soon as the semolino cools, add the cream and thoroughly mix together.

Line an oven tray with baking paper. Optionally, you can soak the paper lightly in tap water, crumple it up and set it on the tray's walls. Pour in the mixture until an even level is formed.

Bake at 180° for about 55/60 minutes.

A delightfully tasty cake prepared around Carnevale. Its name comes, supposedly, from the millet (it: "Miglio") flour that our ancestors used to make it.

INGREDIENTS
for a 24 cm Cake

- 500 ML MILK;
- 500 ML WATER;
- 250 GR SEMOLINA;
- 400 GR SHEEP'S MILK RICOTTA;
- 200 GR SUGAR;
- 5 EGGS;
- 25 GR BUTTER;
- 1 ORANGE AND LEMON ZEST;
- VANILLA EXTRACT;
- A PINCH OF CINNAMON;
- ORANGE BLOSSOM WATER.

Zeppole di Assunta con le Patate
(Fried Dough with added Potatoes)

INGREDIENTS

for 40 Donuts

- 1 KG TYPE 00 FLOUR;
- 800 GR POTATOES;
- 150 GR SUGAR;
- 2 SACHETS VANILLIN;
- A PINCH OF SALT;
- 200 GR BUTTER;
- 5/6 MEDIUM EGGS;
- 2 FRESH YEAST CUBES, 25 GR EACH;
- 1 LEMON ZEST;
- FRYING OIL.

Carefully clean and blanch the potatoes, without peeling them first. After about 20 minutes, check if they're done by poking them with a fork: if it goes inside without much resistance, they're ready. Take them out of the water, cool for a while, then peel and crush in a potato masher.

Pour the flour on your pastry board, or other work surface, to form a mound. Dig a little cavity on top, add in the two crushed yeast cubes, sugar, the mashed potato, softened (but not melted) butter, lemon zest, a pinch of salt and finally the two sachets of vanillin.

Start kneading, gradually adding the contents of an egg, until the dough becomes elastic.

Let the dough sit until it doubles in size then, without moving it around too much, cut some chunks off with a kitchen scraper. Shape those pieces into small sausages, about 20 cm long and 1 cm thick, then close them up in a "ribbon" shape, uniting the two extremities and lightly pressing on the joint to "seal" it.

Let the zeppole grow on a clean cloth, and cover them with a towel. They don't have to grow fully, only about half an hour, if the temperature is right.

Heat the oil at 170° and try to dip one in. If it sizzles and grows, then the oil is at the right temperature.

Keep the oil at the same heat, and continue frying until they're done. Drain the excess oil on cooking paper and then, still hot, dip them in sugar until completely covered.

I usually prepare two bags: one with sugar, a pinch of cinnamon, a sachet of vanillin; the other with the same ingredients, plus a bit of powdered sugar. I start by dipping the zeppola in the first bag and shaking, so that the mixture absorbs the remaining oil; then, once it's a bit dryer, I dip it in the second bag, so that the sugar doesn't stain with oil.

This recipe is called "le zeppole di Assunta" (Assunta's Zeppole) for the simple reason that it belongs to an old acquantaince of my mother's, Assunta, who used to be our neighbour and always gave us some to enjoy when she made them.

We already mentioned part of the history of this recipe before, when I described the neapolitan version of Krapfen, which make use of blanched potatoes to soften up the doughnut and give the dessert a sweeter hue.

✳ ✳ ✳

Pastiera di Pasta *(Pasta Cake)*

Boil water and a pinch of salt in a large pot, then tip in the pasta. Pour in some cold water to halt the boiling right before draining, then place inside a large tin.

Whisk the eggs in a bowl with sugar and all the different aromas, then add the candied citron, minced, and finally the milk. Pour the mixture in the tin with the spaghetti and mix together carefully.

Bake in a 180° oven for about 50/60 minutes, until the surface is a crispy brown. Cool, then take it out of the mould, slice it and serve on a platter with a sprinkle of powdered sugar on top.

I think that the pastiera di pasta is a typical dessert of my town, Torre del Greco: even though it's possible to find it pretty much everywhere around the Vesuvius, it's much more common in the bakeries of the so called "Golden Mile". It could be considered the sweeter sister of the fried pizza di pasta that's so prevalent in Naples: its preparation is very similar, except for the addition of sugar, candied fruit and flower extracts, which give it a wonderful perfume and a very sweet taste.

INGREDIENTS

for a 22 cm wide Cake

- 500 GR SPAGHETTI "CAPELLINI";
- 400 GR SUGAR;
- 8 EGGS;
- 500 ML MILK;
- 1 VIAL WILDFLOWER EXTRACT;
- 1 VIAL ORANGE BLOSSOM WATER;
- 1 LEMON ZEST, GRATED;
- 100 GR CANDIED FRUITS;
- A PINCH OF CINNAMON;
- POWDERED SUGAR.

Delizia al Limone *(Lemon Delight)*

INGREDIENTS

for 9 delights

FOR THE SPONGE CAKE

- 300 GR SUGAR;
- 300 GR FLOUR;
- 300 GR EGG WHITES;
- 150 GR EGG YOLKS;
- 1 SORRENTO LEMON;

FOR THE LEMON CREAM

- 200 GR EGG YOLKS;
- 200 GR SUGAR;
- 200 GR BUTTER;
- 200 ML WATER;
- 20 GR ISINGLASS;
- 1 LEMON;
- 50 ML LIMONCELLO;
- 500 ML FRESH
  WHIPPED CREAM;
- 50 GR POWDERED SUGAR;
- 2 GRATED LEMON ZESTS;

FOR THE LIMONCELLO SYRUP

- 100 ML WATER;
- 100 GR SUGAR;
- 1 LEMON;
- 150 ML LIMONCELLO;
- 1 LEMON ZEST.

Start with the sponge cake. Whisk the egg whites with 150 grams of sugar until they form peaks. Then beat the egg yolks with another 150 grams of sugar for at least 10 minutes. When the two mixtures are ready, gently combine them in a large bowl. Add in the flour, which you will have already filtered, and the grated lemon zest; pour the resulting mixture in 7-8 cm wide half-sphere moulds. Bake in pre-heated oven at 180° for about 20 minutes. Take them out of the oven, let cool a bit, then take the sponge cakes out of the moulds and finish cooling on a wire rack.

For the cream, start by soaking the isinglass in a bowl of cold water for 10 minutes. Pour some water in a small pot, together with the grated zest of two lemons; add the sugar in and melt. As soon as the mixture is boiling, turn off the heat and leave to infuse until it cools completely.

Strain the mixture and put it on the stove again. When it's gotten warm again, pour it in a bowl with the whisked egg yolks. Whisk everything together, and then add in a small pot, which you'll put on low heat. Simmer while gently stirring. As soon as it reaches boiling point, add the diced butter, mix together and cook for 2-3 minutes.

Now add the soaked isinglass, thoroughly squeezed, and limoncello. Mesh together, then turn off the heat and pour the resulting mixture in a low, wide tin. Cover the cream's surface with cling film and store in the fridge until completely cold.

Now on to the syrup: place sugar and water in a pot, add the limoncello and some grated lemon zest, then bring to boil. Cool the resulting syrup in the fridge and then strain it to remove all the small chunks of zest. Place it in a vaporizer or a blender.

Take out the lemon cream from the fridge and, if it's firm and gelatinous, mix it in a blender to give it a creamy, smooth texture. Mix the whipped cream and powdered sugar together, reserve 3 scoops for later use and then combine the rest with the lemon cream.

If the cream isn't completely smooth, then strain it, pressing it down with a spatula; the clumps should disappear, and the overall texture should stay unaltered.

Take the sponge cake half-spheres and empty them from the flat side, then lightly soak them in syrup and fill with lemon cream. Close up the cavity with the flat crust you cut. Dilute the remaining lemon cream with milk or single cream and then use it to cover the spheres, after soaking them with syrup on the outside, too.

Garnish with a spoonful of whipped cream and some lemon zest. Leave in the fridge for a few hours

* * *

Sfogliatelle Frolle *(Pastry filled with Choux)*

Mix the flour with lard until the latter is completely absorbed. Add the other ingredients and knead quickly, then roll into a ball, which you will cover with plastic wrap and let rest in the fridge for a few hours.

Prepare the filling by combining ricotta, sugar, vanilla and cinnamon. Bring a pot of water to boil with a pinch of salt, then sprinkle the semolina in. Cook and stir continuously for 10 minutes, then pour the mixture in a bowl and cool completely.

Once cool, combine with the ricotta cream, eggs and candied fruit, mixing until it's a uniform cream.

Partition the dough in many little balls, which you will roll out in 5 cm wide ovals. Place a portion of cream in the center of every oval, then close it, putting a light pressure on the edges. Cut it with a round dough cutter, then place on a parchment-lined oven tray. Brush with some egg yolk and bake at 180° for 15/18 minutes.

Cool, and once warm, dust with powdered sugar.

INGREDIENTS
for 30 Frolle

FOR THE DOUGH:

- 1 KG TYPE 00 FLOUR;
- 400 GR LARD;
- 350 GR SUGAR;
- 2 EGGS;
- 13 GR HONEY;
- ½ TSP. AMMONIA FOR CAKES;

FOR THE FILLING

- 250 GR SEMOLINA;
- 400 GR SHEEP'S MILK RICOTTA;
- 2 EGGS;
- 700 GR WATER;
- 100 GR CANDIED FRUIT;
- 2 SACHETS VANILLIN;
- A PINCH OF CINNAMON;
- POWDERED SUGAR Q.S.

Sfogliatelle Ricce *(Clam-shaped Puff Pastry)*

INGREDIENTS

for 30 Ricce

FOR THE SHORT PASTRY

- 500 GR TYPE 00 FLOUR;
- 250 GR LARD;
- 200 GR WATER;
- A PINCH OF SALT;
- 15 GR HONEY.

FOR THE FILLING

- 125 GR SEMOLINA;
- 200 GR SHEEP'S MILK RICOTTA;
- 1 EGG;
- 350 GR WATER;
- 50 GR CANDIED FRUIT;
- 1 SACHET VANILLIN;
- A PINCH OF CINNAMON;
- POWDERED SUGAR.

Mix the flour with water, honey and a pinch of salt. Work the dough, very energetically, until you get a smooth bun; wrap it in plastic and leave to rest for a few hours.

Roll out the dough as thin as you can, maybe with the help of a pasta maker, forming a layer that's 20 cm long.

Roll the dough from one end, brushing the outside with lard. Roll until it's tight, then once again cover the outside surface with lard. Let rest in the fridge for at least 12 hours.

Prepare the filling by mixing ricotta, sugar, vanilla and cinnamon. Bring to boil a pot of water with a pinch of salt, then sprinkle the semolina in.

Cook while stirring for 10 minutes, then pour the mixture in a bowl and cool completely. Once cool, add in the ricotta cream, the egg and the candied fruit, mixing until you get a uniform cream.

Take the dough out of the fridge and cut it in 1 cm thick slices: the so-called "tappo" ("cap"). Use your thumb to make an impression on the center, going towards the outside, until you get a bell-like cone shape.

Fill with a spoonful of filling, and press the edges together to close it up.

Bake at 180° for 30/35 minutes or until completely brown. Serve cold, dusted with powdered sugar.

It's not at all surprising that many verses were dedicated to this world-class pastry.

As many other Neapolitan desserts, sfogliatelle originated in a convent, where the nuns often had to come up with good recipes using what was available to them, which wasn't usually much, sometimes even trading with the outside world to recoup some of their monetary losses.

It seems that this particular dessert was created back in 1600 in the convent of Santa Rosa, on the Amalfi Coast, by mixing together custard and sour cherries. It soon became a favourite in the area, which means that it often saw use as an object of trade.

It later reached Naples thanks to the efforts of an innkeeper-turned-baker called Pasquale Pintauro, who impressed his own variations on the filling and crust, creating what we know today as the "sfogliatella sisters", Frolla and Riccia, even though the original Santa Rosa recipe is still in use today.

Deliziose *(Custard and Hazelnut Filled Short Pastry Cookies)*

INGREDIENTS

- 250 GR TYPE 00 FLOUR;
- 2 EGGS;
- 100 GR POWDERED SUGAR;
- 80 ML EVO OIL;
- 12 GR BAKING POWDER;
- 1 SACHET VANILLIN;

FOR THE CUSTARD

- 500 ML MILK;
- 50 GR FLOUR;
- 4 EGG YOLKS;
- 150 GR SUGAR;
- 1 SACHET VANILLIN;
- AS GARNISH:
- 100 GR CHOPPED HAZELNUTS OR SHAVED CHOCOLATE;
- POWDERED SUGAR.

Mix all the dry ingredients on your work surface: flour, powdered sugar, baking powder and vanillin, then add the eggs, beat with a fork and start kneading.

Gradually incorporate the oil until you get a smooth, uniform dough. Wrap the dough bun in film and let it rest in the fridge for at least a few hours.

Prepare the custard: fill a pot with milk and add vanillin. Heat for a few minutes, then take it off. Whisk the egg yolks and sugar in a bowl, using an electric blender. Add flour and vanillin. Combine this mixture with the milk you warmed up earlier, then bring it to boil in a small pot (set the heat on low and stir continuously with a wooden ladle).

Turn off the heat when you think the cream has reached the right texture (we usually turn it off 2 or 3 minutes after the milk starts boiling).

Cool the cream at ambient temperature, covered with a cloth.

Roll out the dough with a pin, until you get a layer a few millimeters thick. Using a round dough cutter of about 5 cm (or really, whichever round object you can get your hands on, like a glass), carve out round shapes.

Let the cookies cool, and then stuff one of dough circles with custard. Cover it with another circle. Put a little pressure on top to let the cream stick to both circles.

Top up the deliziose with a sprinkle of chocolate chips on the sides (or chopped hazelnuts, if you want) and a dusting of powdered sugar on top.

Struffoli *(Honey Balls)*

Mix together all the ingredients until you get a dough that's not too soft, wrap it in film and let rest for an hour in the fridge. Afterwards, prepare many thin sticks, working with little or (if you can) no flour, then cut in small pieces and fry in hot oil. As soon as a batch's done, pluck it out of the oil with a skimmer and drain on absorbing cooking paper.

Melt sugar, vanillin and honey in a pot of water. Add the struffoli a little at a time and stir them inside the liquid. Take them out when they're sufficiently "shined" and place them on a platter. Sprinkle some toppings before placing other struffoli on top. Continue layering struffoli, candied fruit, sprinkles and chocolate chips.

The Neapolitan Struffolo is easy to find in the South, maybe with a different name or a slight variation on the topping. It seems to be Greek in origin, which you may guess due to the heavy-handed use of honey. The simple ingredients and process, but mainly the possibility of keeping them fresh for quite a long time, has allowed this recipe to survive through the ages to the present day.

INGREDIENTS

FOR THE DOUGH

- 1 KG TYPE 00 FLOUR;
- 100 GR SUGAR;
- 80 GR BUTTER;
- 50 GR RHUM;
- 8 EGGS;
- 1 SACHET VANILLIN;
- 5 GR SALT;
- A PINCH OF YEAST POWDER;
- 2 TBSP. OIL;

FOR THE TOPPING

- 100 GR WATER;
- 200 GR SUGAR;
- 250 GR HONEY;
- 1 SACHET VANILLIN.
- OTHER TOPPINGS:
- 200 GR CANDIED FRUIT;
- 200 GR SPRINKLES;
- 100 GR WHITE SUGARED ALMONDS WITH CINNAMON;
- 20 CANDIED CHERRIES, WHOLE;
- 100 GR CHOCOLATE CHIPS.

Crostata di Frutta Fresca *(Fresh Fruit Tart)*

INGREDIENTS

for a 28 cm Cake

SHORT PASTRY

- 300 GR FLOUR;
- 150 GR BUTTER;
- 2 EGGS;
- 150 GR SUGAR;
- A PINCH OF SALT;
- GRATED LEMON ZEST;
- 1 SACHET VANILLIN;
- CUSTARD;
- 4 EGG YOLKS;
- 100 GR CASTER SUGAR;
- 20 GR FLOUR;
- 20 GR CORN STARCH;
- ½ LT WHOLE MILK;
- VANILLA EXTRACT;
- GRATED LEMON ZEST;

FOR THE TOPPING

- 3 BANANAS;
- 2 KG ASSORTED SEASON FRUIT;
- FOR THE GLAZE:
- 50 GR APRICOT JELLY.

Prepare the short pastry by quickly mixing flour, butter, eggs, sugar, salt, lemon zest and vanillin. Wrap the resulting bun in cling film and let sit in the fridge for a few hours.

Now on to the cream. Whisk together the yolks with sugar. add flour, vanilla extract and warm milk spiced up with some lemon zest.

Place the mixture in a pot and turn the heat on low, stirring continuously for about 5 minutes. Take it off the heat and continue stirring to cool, then store with some cling film touching the surface, so that it doesn't get crusty.

Transfer the pastry to a 28 cm pie dish, which you will have already coated in butter.

Bake at 180° until the pastry colours lightly, then line it with a sheet of baking paper (and some chickpeas on top), so that it keeps its even shape and raised edges. After about 15 minutes, remove the baking paper and continue browning for 4/5 minutes. Take it out of the oven and cool.

It's time to fill our crostata. Spread a layer of custard on the pastry, then cover that layer with thin banana slices. Top with your season fruits of choice, cut and arranged to be as aesthetically pleasing as you like.

Finishing touch: warm up the apricot jelly and gently brush the surface of the pie.

Torta Ricotta e Pera *(Pear Ricotta Cake)*

Prepare the sponge, energetically whisking the egg whites with a pinch of salt and powdered sugar, until they form a uniform, fluffy mixture. Once ready, gently pour in the chopped hazelnuts.

Split the mixture in two identical halves, and put them in two different 24 cm pie dishes, which you will have previously lined with baking paper. Cook at 140° for an hour.

Once ready, take the dishes out of the oven and remove the paper immediately.

Check if the two discs fit into the springform pan you'll use to assemble the cake. If not, trim the edges a bit, now that the meringue is still hot and malleable.

Prepare the cream, melting the caster sugar in 30 gr of water. Whisk the egg whites until they form peaks, gently adding in some syrup from the tinned pears. Whisk the ricotta with a spoon to get it nice and creamy, then add the beaten eggs, diced pears, isinglass (previously soaked in cold water and melted in a pot) and, finally, the whipped cream with powdered sugar.

Assemble the cake by placing one of two discs on the bottom of a 24 cm springform pan, layer with cream and then top with the other disc.

Let it sit in the fridge for 2 hours, then dust with powdered sugar.

It is in the magical land of Amalfi that the ricotta cake was born… but only fairly recently, thanks to a local prominent figure in the field of bakery. Which means that this isn't really a "traditional" recipe, although the practice of mixing ricotta and pears goes back to the farmers of old, who always made use of simple, everyday ingredients. It's to be said that this cake, as delicate and pleasant as it is, has seen tremendous success in recent years, to the point that it can easily be found in many of our bakeries.

INGREDIENTS
for a 24 cm wide Cake

FOR THE HAZELNUT SPONGE

- 120 GR EGG WHITES;
- 120 GR CHOPPED HAZELNUT KERNELS;
- 120 GR POWDERED SUGAR;
- FOR THE CREAM:
- 300 GR SHEEP'S MILK RICOTTA;
- 75 GR SUGAR;
- 1 MEDIUM EGG WHITE;
- 250 GR TINNED PEARS;
- 300 GR WHIPPED CREAM;
- 20 GR POWDERED SUGAR;
- 6 GR ISINGLASS.

Fiocchi di Neve *(Snowflakes) (Cream-filled Fluffy Pastries)*

INGREDIENTS

for about 25 Snowflakes

- 250 GR MANITOBA FLOUR;
- 100 ML MILK;
- 1 EGG;
- 50 GR BUTTER;
- 50 GR SUGAR;
- 12 GR FRESH BREWER'S YEAST;
- A PINCH OF SALT.

FOR THE CREAM:

- 250 ML MILK;
- 50 GR SUGAR;
- 25 GR TYPE 00 FLOUR;
- 200 GR SHEEP'S MILK RICOTTA;
- 25 GR POWDERED SUGAR;
- 200 ML WHIPPED CREAM.

Prepare the white cream. Put the sifted flour and sugar in a small pot, whisk and very slowly pour in the milk while stirring, to avoid clumps.

Cook on low heat, while stirring continuously, until the mixture thickens, then cool.

Strain the ricotta and combine with powdered sugar in a bowl. Add the milk cream you prepared before and mix together. Add the whipped cream, a little at a time, mixing with a spoon moving from the bottom to the top, until you get a white, smooth cream. Let it sit in the fridge.

For the brioche dough, pour the warm milk into a bowl, crumble the yeast, add sugar and mix together. Let the mixture rest for 20 minutes, than add the beaten egg, sifted flour and salt, and start mixing by hand. The resulting dough will be quite sticky. When it's well-mixed, start adding some diced butter, a little at a time.

Liberally flour your work surface, place the mixture on top and work it, with the help of a sprinkling of flour, into a smooth, uniform dough. Cover in plastic wrap, then with a cloth, and let it sit until it doubles in size. After leavening, split the dough in many 30 gr chunks, and roll each one into a ball, then place them on a parchment-lined oven tray(and make sure there's a lot of wiggle room between them).

Let them rest in a warm spot until, once again, they grow to double their size.

Bake in a preheated 180° oven for about 15 minutes, until they're golden brown. Cool, then, with a bismark-tipped piping bag, fill the snowflakes while still warm.

Dust each snowflake with plenty of powdered sugar, then place them on a platter and store in the fridge, ready to be served.

In stark opposition to the centuries-old pastry recipes in Neapolitan cuisine, the Snowflake is a recent "discovery", invented by a baker from the Naples city centre. It's a simple little dessert that, nonetheless, met great success due to its delicious taste (not to mention the viral marketing campaign on social media).

It's for all intents and purposes a fluffy brioche filled with milk-based cream, an archetype that's found, with some slight differences, in Sicilian cuisine.

* * *

Panettone Prestofatto *(Readymade Panettone)*

Whisk the eggs together with sugar, then add oil, a pinch of salt, the grated lemon zest and then the sifted flour. Melt the yeast in a cup of milk and pour it in the mixture. Butter and liberally flour an oven tray with raised edges and bake at 180° for 35/40 minutes, without ever opening the oven door.

Mix the egg white with powdered sugar, being careful not to use too much white as that would water down the mixture.

Take the cake out of the oven a few minutes before its planned cooking time and top with the meringue you just prepared and some sprinkles. Put it back in and bake until done. Use a stick or a long toothpick to determine if it's cooked on the inside, then let it sit in the oven off to slowly cool until all the meringue on top is dry.

My nana, not really what you'd call a Michelin star chef, often employed this tested recipe to keep her nephews and nieces quiet as they bounced around the house in long winter nights. I gather it took her hours to bake it, busy as she was with housekeeping, but it was simply so good that I still remember it fondly.

INGREDIENTS

for a 28 cm wide, 6 cm tall Cake

- 300 GR TYPE 00 FLOUR;
- 100 ML MILK;
- 5 EGGS;
- 150 GR OIL;
- 200 GR SUGAR;
- 1 SACHET YEAST POWDER;
- A PINCH OF SALT;
- 1 GRATED LEMON ZEST;
- FOR THE TOPPING:
- 1 EGG WHITE;
- 150 GR POWDERED SUGAR;
- COLOURED SPRINKLES.

"Did you eat?' is the most authentic expression of love."

Laura Morante

Sweets, Pastries, Salty and Sweet Cookies

"I hate a man who swallows his food, affecting not to know what he is eating. I suspect his taste in higher matters."

Charles Lamb

Sweets, Pastries, Salty and Sweet Cookies

When you're around Naples and hear someone (usually an older gentleman) say "Na guantiera 'e pastarelle" ("a tray of pastries"), it's used to refer to all the pastries, almond cakes and cookies that we enjoy during house parties, gatherings that happen between four familiar walls in lieu of restaurants and other fine dining establishments, where celebrations are wild and a good time is had by all. In the past, certain pastries and cookies were closely tied to feasts, and were especially and only made during those times, such as the rococò, the susamielli and the quaresimali, in addition to those little treats we used to prepare every day for the morning break, in place of pre-packaged snacks. Just the smell was enough to fill your belly, and it was all too hard to wait for the cookies to cool before trying to get a taste.

Our traditional taralli, especially those with lard and ground pepper, are still regularly served with a nice glass of wine or beer, ideally on a balcony with a good view of the open sea or from a local belvedere in summer. It's getting increasingly rare to find homemade taralli, but given the chance and enough time, it's worth it to try your hand at the recipe.

- Biscotti Quaresimali (Lenten Cookies with Almonds)
- Paste di Mandorla (Almond Dough Cookies)
- Roccocò (Donut-Shaped Almond Cookies)
- Susamielli ("S"-Shaped Almond Cookies)
- Biscotti all'Amarena (Sour Cherry Cookies)
- Taralli Sugna e Pepe (Taralli with Lard and Ground Pepper)

Biscotti Quaresimali *(Lenten Cookies with Almonds)*

INGREDIENTS

- 500 GR TYPE 00 FLOUR;
- 8 GR INSTANT YEAST POWDER;
- 400 GR SUGAR;
- 50 GR EVO OIL;
- 4 EGGS;
- 150 GR TOASTED HAZELNUTS;
- 150 GR TOASTED ALMONDS;
- 50 GR DICED CANDIED FRUIT;
- A FEW DROPS OF VANILLA EXTRACT;
- A PINCH OF CINNAMON POWDER;
- A PINCH OF NUTMEG;
- A PINCH OF SALT.

Combine flour, eggs, oil, sugar, extracts, salt and yeast on a work surface and start mixing together, until you get a uniform dough. Add hazelnuts, almonds and candied fruit, and knead to spread them evenly. The resulting dough will be sticky: with the help of a little flour, take some small chunks off and shape into a stick about 2/3 cm thick.

Line a few oven trays with sheets of baking paper, place the sticks at an even distance from each other and brush with some egg yolk. Bake at 170/180° for 15/16 minutes with ventilated oven. As soon as they're done, cool and slice diagonally. Each slice should be about 2 cm wide. Bake again at 180° for 10/12 minutes, always keeping them at a certain distance from each other so that both sides cook evenly. Always check during cooking, and take out when lightly browned.

They keep fresh for a few days, if we store them inside a closed bag. Enjoy dipped in vinsanto or limoncello.

Neapolitan tradition dictates that Quaresimali be prepared the day before the start of Lent, the Holy Wednesday, and that's where the Quaresimali (Lent is Quaresima in Italian) get their name. Technically, you shouldn't eat animal fats during Lent. Practically, I always add something, in this case a drizzle of EVO oil, to soften the dough.

You can find almost the same cookies in central Italy- ours differ mainly in the use of candied fruit and our favourite extracts, that we often use to bake other types of cookie, like cinnamon, nutmeg, coriander and anise.

Paste di Mandorla *(Almond Dough Cookies)*

Bake the almonds whole at 80/90° for 15/20 minutes, so that they dry up a bit. Cool, then chop finely, maybe sprinkling with a bit of sugar to try and make them as thin as possible. Finely chop the candied orange zest too; you could even crush them with a pestle and make cream.

Now, on to the cookies. Pour the almond flour in a bowl and add the other ingredients, starting with a little egg white and mixing. How much egg white should be added depends on the density of the almond flour and how much white it manages to absorb. If you find that the resulting dough is a bit too hard, add a little more egg white.

Now you can either put the mixture inside a piping bag or work it by hand. In the first case, just squeeze the mixture on a parchment-lined oven tray, shaping each cookie into a little mound. In the latter case, roll into a little ball using your palms. Top with a single almond, a candied fruit or a coffee bean. Store in the fridge overnight. The following day bake at about 180/200° for 7/8 minutes, making sure that they only brown on the outside. Baking the cookies correctly is essential for a good outcome. The cookies, at the end, must be brown on the outside and still quite soft on the inside.

It's custom to call these cookies "pastarelle" ("little pastries"). They're usually round or clam-shaped with different tastes, and they were a favourite during house parties, usually paired with a glass of sweet wine, vermouth or limoncello.

INGREDIENTS

- 1 KG ALMOND KERNELS;
- 800 GR SUGAR;
- 200 GR CANDIED ORANGE ZEST;
- 50 GR ACACIA HONEY;
- 250 GR EGG WHITE.

Roccocò *(Donut-shaped Almond Cookies)*

INGREDEINTS

for about 30 Cookies

- 1 KG FLOUR;
- 800 GR SUGAR;
- 600 GR TOASTED, PEELED ALMONDS;
- 20 GR PISTO;
- 5 GR BAKING AMMONIA;
- 2 SACHETS VANILLIN;
- 300 GR WATER;
- 1 LEMON ZEST;
- 125 GR ORANGE ZEST;
- 125 GR CITRON;
- 3 GR CINNAMON;
- 1 EGG YOLK.

Heat the water with a lemon zest for about 10 minutes. Once cool, it can be used to make the dough. Toast the almonds for about 15/20 minutes in a preheated oven at 80/90°, then cool and chop roughly, you should aim for adequately-sized chunks or even whole almonds.

Mix all the dry ingredients, then the orange zest and citron, then finally add water and start kneading vigorously. The resulting dough will be firm and sticky. Grease your hands, to avoid any dough sticking to them, and take some chunks off the dough, forming some sticks about 2 cm wide and 20 cm long. Join the extremities in the shape of a circle/donut.

Place the donuts on a parchment-lined oven tray, leaving some much needed space in between to avoid creating little cookie chimeras. Applying a little pressure, place some whole almonds on the top surface of the donut, within about 1 cm of each other. Brush with egg yolk and bake in a preheated oven at 170° for 15/18 minutes.

During baking, first they'll grow and then go flat. They're ready once the part that's brushed with yolk is fully browned, while the cookie dough is a lighter, golden hue.

They'll still be a little soft when you take them out of the oven, so wait a few minutes before prying them from the paper.

Pisto is a herb mixture that you can make yourself with cinnamon, coriander, cloves, nutmeg and anise, in case you can't find it in your local shops.

Susamielli *(S-Shaped Almond Cookies)*

Liberally flour your work surface, then place all the dry ingredients on top, along with the orange and tangerine zest. Add the honey, after melting it in a pot, then start mixing all the ingredients together. Wrap the resulting dough bun in cling film and let it sit in the fridge for about 30 minutes. Cut the dough into chunks and mould each one into a 15/16 long cylinder. Shape each cylinder into an "S". Place all the cookies on a parchment-lined oven tray and bake at 180° for about 15/18 minutes. Cool the susamielli on a wire rack before storing them.

Susamielli are traditional Neapolitan Christmas cookies. They sport a characteristic "S" shape and their origin is really, really ancient. Susamielli used to be prepared, in the old days, with sesame and honey, and their name is supposedly a portmanteau of these ingredients (it. sesamo e miele). They're also called "Sapienze" sometimes, due to the fact that the nuns of the Santa Maria della Sapienza Convent were specialized in the making of this recipe.

Speaking of which, the recipe for susamielli figures in the 1788 cookbook from chef V. Corrado, under the name of "susamielli nobili" (noble susamielli). The reason for this is that, back then, there were three different variants of susamielli, each destined for either nobles or peasants: the "susamielli nobili" were baked using top-quality white flour; the "susamielli dello zampognaro" were usually served to bagpipe players (that is literally what "zampognaro" means, as the zampogna is a kind of bagpipe) and were usually baked with rough flour and recycled ingredients; the "susamielli del buon cammino" (lit. "susamielli of the righteous path") were instead reserved for priests and friars. Today, the recipe for susamielli nobili is the most used. Susamielli, like roccocò, are scented with the so-called pisto, a mix of spices typically prepared with cinnamon, cloves, nutmeg and coriander.

INGREDIENTS
for about 30 Cookies

- 750 GR TYPE 00 FLOUR;
- 250 GR SUGAR;
- 300 GR PEELED, TOASTED ALMONDS;
- 20 GR PISTO;
- 5 GR BAKING AMMONIA;
- 2 SACHETS VANILLIN;
- 750 GR HONEY;
- 2 GRATED ORANGE ZEST;
- 1 FINELY DICED TANGERINE ZEST;
- 1 EGG YOLK.

Biscotti all'Amarena *(Sour Cherry Cookies)*

INGREDIENTS

for about 20 cookies

FOR THE SHORT PASTRY

- 400 GR TYPE 00 FLOUR;
- 2 EGGS;
- 180 GR BUTTER;
- 220 GR SUGAR;
- 16 GR YEAST POWDER.

FOR THE FILLING

- 400 GR SPONGE CAKE;
- 250 GR SOUR CHERRY JAM;
- 2 TBSP. BITTER COCOA POWDER;
- 30 GR FINELY CHOPPED PEANUTS;
- ½ SHOT GLASS STREGA;

ALTERNATIVELY

- 400 GR LADYFINGERS;
- 300 GR JAM;
- 2 TBSP. BITTER COCOA POWDER;
- 30 GR CHOPPED PEANUTS;
- ½ SHOT GLASS STREGA;
- WATER Q.S.

FOR THE GLAZE

- 1 EGG WHITE;
- 100 GR POWDERED SUGAR.

Start by preparing the short pastry, mixing flour with butter until it's completely absorbed. Add all the other ingredients and knead vigorously, then split it in two dough buns, wrap it in film and let it sit in the fridge for a few hours.

For the filling, we can either use some leftover sponge cake or ladyfingers as main ingredient. Either way, mix with a bit of lightly melted jam, peanuts, bitter cocoa and Strega liquor. The dough has to be firm and uniform; use a stand mixer if you have to.

Roll out the short pastry on a work surface until you get an even layer that's about half a cm thin. Cut it into rectangles. Take a dollop of filling, about as long as the pastry you just cut, and place it on top of the rectangle. Join the two extremities on top and gently overlap them, leaving the long sides open. Then, turn it over with the dough's joint left under, and slightly press on top to seal the deal.

Cut the cookies with a knife and place them on an oven tray, with the "joint" still on the underside.

Brush the pastries with some meringue, prepared by whisking together egg white and sugar until they form peaks, and then engrave some horizontal lines on top using a sour cherry jam-tinted toothpick.

Bake in a preheated oven at 200° for a quick cooking, no more than 5 minutes so that they don't get misshapen, then lower the heat to 180° and cook for about 10/12 minutes. Cool completely and remove from the tray. They keep fresh for quite a while if stored in a well-sealed bag.

The history of this pastry, one of the tastier treats we have ever made, says it all on the "Neapolitan character". The original recipe for the filling is entirely dependent on the leftovers of a pastry laboratory, which are always plenty, as per our long standing tradition to never throw anything in the bin. Who knows, maybe we could make cookies with it.

Taralli Sugna e Pepe
(Taralli with Lard and Ground Pepper)

Melt the yeast in a pot of warm water with a teaspoon of sugar and one of honey. Roughly chop the almonds.

Combine all the ingredients in a large bowl and mix, first in the bowl, and then on a work surface, until you get a uniform dough bun. Knead the bun for at least 10/15 minutes, after which let rest for a few hours, until it doubles in size.

Afterwards, knead the dough a little more and then divide it in many pieces of about 40 gr each. Work each one into sticks about 20 cm long, then braid two together at a time. Close each braid into a "donut" shape. Garnish with whole almonds, placed at random in the dough.

Spread the taralli on a parchment-lined oven tray and let them sit for at least another hour. After they've once again doubled in size, bake at 180° for about 40 minutes, until they're nice and brown.

As with the other recipes in this section, taralli can be kept fresh for days if tightly sealed.

Always great disciples of our oft-mentioned long-standing tradition of not wasting a single thing, the bakers of Naples "discovered" a new way to recycle stale bread by mixing it with lard and pepper, giving taralli a decisive taste and creating a sort of "bread for the poor", being both cheap and very nutritious. Then, in the 19ᵗʰ century, almonds were added to the classic "lard and pepper" recipe, becoming the taralli we know and love today.

Even Pino Daniele, the famous bluesman, celebrated the deliciousness of taralli with his song "Fortunato", dedicated to Fortunato Bisaccia (Fortunato o' Tarallaro). A known figure in the 70s and 80s, Fortunato travelled all over the city with his little barrow, selling Taralli to anyone in need of a bellyful.

INGREDIENTS
for about 20 Taralli

- 500 GR TYPE 00 FLOUR;
- 200 GR LARD;
- 25 GR BREWER'S YEAST;
- 200 GR UNPEELED ALMONDS;
- 2 TBSP. GROUND BLACK PEPPER;
- 150 ML WATER;
- 1 TSP. HONEY;
- 12 GR SALT.

"*Tis an ill cook that cannot lick his own fingers.*"

William Shakespeare

Liquors

"In case I die, bring me some coffee. You'll see,
I'll come back to life like a modern day Lazarus."

Eduardo de Filippo, *"Fantasmi a Roma"*

Liquors

Lemon farming has always been a point of pride for many Campanians, the fruits flourishing in a bright palette of colours on the terraces of our coasts. Walnuts, too, are grown in large quantities in many different areas. Both make up the base ingredients of good liquor, made during certain times of the year with the methods detailed in ancient recipes. Waiting for the right season is essential, since the fruits have to be ripe enough to be macerated in alcohol. Here, too, the advice passed down through the ages helps us consistently create a good enough product.

- Limoncello
- Nocillo

Limoncello

INGREDIENTS

- 1 LT 90° ALCOHOL;
- 1 LT WATER;
- 800 GR SUGAR;
- 6 OR 7 UNTREATED LARGE LEMONS, OF WHICH ONE GREEN.

Wash and dry the lemons, peel the zest and keep only the yellow part (as the white part could be too bitter), which you will soak in alcohol for about 5 days, in a large jar with a cork.

Keep the jar in a spot without a lot of light, maybe covered with a cloth.

After the five days have passed, prepare the syrup by boiling a pot of water mixed with sugar. Let it stew for just a few minutes, then cool. Pour in the alcohol infusion, filtering it through a narrow mesh strainer.

Bottle the contents and store in a cupboard. It needs to rest for about a month before developing its characteristic taste.

It's said that, as early as the 20th century, the rich families of Sorrento and Amalfi offered a taste of this wonderful, traditional liquor to their guests; others instead say that the Limoncello dates as far back as the Saracen invasions, made by fishermen and farmers, who sipped it in the morning as a much needed reprieve from the cold; others still maintain that the spirit was invented in a friar monastery.

Nocillo

A valuable walnut-based liquor produced in the Vesuvian area, mostly thanks to the many centuries-old, traditional walnut plantations.

Clean and dry the walnuts, split them in quarters and infuse in alcohol for about 60 days in a large lidded jug, along with all the other spices. Keep the jug in a place without much light and cover with a towel.

After the 60 days have passed, prepare the syrup by bringing a pot of water and sugar to boil for just a few minutes. Cool and then pour in the alcohol infusion, filtering it through a narrow mesh strainer. Bottle and keep in a cupboard. After a month of rest, it will acquire its characteristic taste.

In Neapolitan folklore, to make a good nocillo, one needed to pick the walnuts on the night of the 24th of June, which is St. John's Day. There are two given explanations for this little ritual: the first, more rational one is that in these days the fruit's sap is more concentrated; the second, which is slightly more fantastical, pins this choice on the fact that the 24th of June used to be the summer solstice in the calendar used before standard Gregorian. In the night where light prevailed over darkness, witches gathered under the walnut trees for the unholy conventions called "sabbaths".

INGREDIENTS

- 24 WALNUTS WITH GREEN HUSK;
- 1 LT 90° ALCOHOL;
- 500 GR SUGAR;
- 1 LT WATER;
- A PINCH OF NUTMEG;
- 3 CLOVES;
- A PINCH OF CINNAMON;
- 20 TOASTED COFFEE BEANS;
- 40 GR STICKS OF LICORICE ROOT;
- 1 WHOLE ORANGE ZEST;
- 1 WHOLE LEMON ZEST.

"They say that 'Tasting whets the appetite', but starving works wonders too."

Totò al Giro d'Italia

Conserves

"E' chiacchiere nun jèncheno a panza"

"Chatter don't fill your belly"

Neapolitan Proverb

Conserves

Keenly aware of his own incapability to enjoy his favourite food all year round, Man has had to get a bit creative in the past when it came to keeping the freshness and taste of prime materials, or even to shape them to his liking. Keeping that in mind, and taking into account the means available to a housewife, the following recipes will seem like a logical conclusion, with their seasonal ingredients and the storage practices involving the usual products, like oil, vinegar, salt, sugar, etc.

Vegetables and fruit inevitably follow the seasons, there are times in the year where meat doesn't taste quite as good, fish catch inevitably varies from month to month, you get the idea. An idea which might seem a bit out of place today, when supermarkets have their stocks full all year, every year. *The word "conserve" has sort of lost its meaning for everyone, except those who want to eat something different even when it can be bought fresh or eat something fresh that's out of season. Although many don't notice or don't want to notice, even those working in the field.*

Conserves are not limited to veggies or fruit: anchovies, tuna and many other fish lend themselves to an easy, even though finicky and time-consuming, storing process. Meat can be conserved too, even though the seasoning is slightly more difficult, but I can guarantee you that the taste is very different when compared to industrially processed food.

In the following pages I will show you the conserve recipes that some families still enjoy making and eating, typically up until Christmas, just like our grandmas made them, with all the care and attention that's fostered by our tradition and convivial family life.

- MELANZANE SOTT'OLIO (EGGPLANTS IN OIL)
- PEPERONI SOTT'OLIO (BELL PEPPERS IN OIL)
- CARCIOFINI SOTT'OLIO (ARTICHOKES IN OIL)
- GIARDINIERA IN AGRODOLCE (SWEET AND SOUR PICKLED VEGETABLES)
- MARMELLATA DI CILIEGIE (CHERRY JAM)

Melanzane Sott'olio *(Eggplants in Oil)*

INGREDIENTS

- 2 KG SMALL-SIZED EGGPLANTS;
- 1 LT WHITE WINE VINEGAR;
- 50 GR FINE SALT;
- 2 CLOVES GARLIC;
- 1 CHILI PEPPER;
- 1 TSP. OREGANO;
- A FEW PEPPERCORNS;
- 500 ML SEED OIL.

Carefully clean and dry the eggplants, peel then cut them in strips of at most 3 or 4 cm in length. Place the strips inside a tin right after cutting, sprinkling with a bit of salt. After completing the cut, dust with the remaining salt and cover using a plate with some kind of weight on top, so that they remain sealed off.

After a few hours their water will drain, and they'll be ready for a quick boiling.

Pour the vinegar in a large pot, bring it to boil and add handfuls of eggplants at a time, which you will have squeezed dry. Give them just a stir and take them out with a skimmer and drain in a large enough colander. You really only have to dip them in vinegar, careful not to overcook as they will get mushy. Wring the eggplant bites through a potato masher to get out the last traces of liquid and place them in a bowl to cool completely. Sprinkle with oregano, minced garlic, chili pepper and some peppercorns, then place them inside glass jars (which you will have already sterilized in boiling water for 20 minutes).

Fill the jars up to 2 cm from the opening, then top up with plenty of oil. Don't let the jars out of sight, you'll have to regularly check the oil level for a few days. Afterwards, put the lid on and store in a dry place, far from the light. They'll be ready to enjoy in about a month.

There's never a shortage of melanzane sott'olio in a true Neapolitan household, because, even if we don't make them, our mother will, our grandma will, our distant cousin five times removed will, the mom and pop store around the corner will, and so on, and so forth. It's one of those things that, in cold winter nights, lets you enjoy a delicious, unique meal with just a side of bread and cheese.

Peperoni Sott'olio *(Bell Peppers in Oil)*

Prepare the brine: in a large pot, combine vinegar, salt and sugar, then carefully stir together and bring to boil for a few minutes. Cool, and in the meantime wash and dry the peppers, remove the stalk and cut in strips at most 1 cm wide, carefully deseeding and cutting out the white parts on the inside.

Once you're done with the cutting, place them in a large tin and pour the cooled brine on top.

Let sit for 48 hours, then drain and dry on a cloth for a few hours more. Place them in another tin and dress with minced garlic, oregano, a light drizzle of oil and chili pepper. Stir vigorously and place them inside sterilized glass jars. Press lightly on top with a wooden ladle to compact, top up with oil, and fill the jar up to a few centimeters from the opening. Cover in oil completely.

Wait a few days before storing them in a cupboard, always to check the oil level. They'll be ready to serve in about 30 days.

The pepper is a vegetable that's easy to pickle, but it's still much more fragile than the eggplant, especially if doused in oil. With this recipe, which comes from our friend Carla, we managed to prepare some great conserves that keep fresh for a long time, even though I'll admit that they're too delicious to last that much.

INGREDIENTS

- 5 KG BELL PEPPERS OF DIFFERENT COLOURS;
- 800 GR SUGAR;
- 250 GR FINE SALT;
- 1 LT SEED OIL;
- 4 CLOVES GARLIC;
- 2 TSP. OREGANO;
- 2 CHILI PEPPERS.

Carciofini sott'olio *(Artichokes in Oil)*

INGREDIENTS

- 2 KG SMALL ARTICHOKES FOR PICKLING;
- 2 LEMONS;
- 1 L WHITE WINE VINEGAR;
- 1 CLOVE GARLIC;
- 1 CHILI PEPPER;
- 1 TSP. OREGANO;
- 500 ML SEED OIL.

Clean and dry the artichokes, remove the outer leaves and peel the stalk. Place them in a large tin filled with water and lemon wedges, which you will squeeze in the same water, and let macerate for a few hours.

After that, drain the artichokes and cook in a pot with vinegar for no more than seven minutes, tipping in after boiling point. Take them out using a skimmer and place them in a colander or wire rack until cool. As soon as they're ready, dress with a drizzle of oil, diced garlic, oregano and chili pepper. Place inside the previously-sterilized glass jars and top up with abundant oil. Check to see if the artichokes are completely covered in oil, then store inside a cupboard. They'll be good to eat in about a month.

This recipe belongs to Nana Raffaella, my mom, who always asks to be there when we make them, ever ready with her advice and recommendations. She's a real stickler about it, to the point that she usually postpones everything to the next day to focus solely on pickling artichokes.

The artichokes themselves must be tiny and fit for pickling, they have to be cleaned, removing just the outer leaves and cut on top, leaving only the soft, meaty part; it's a tried and true ritual, as is the case for the other conserves, too. I think the reason for this is apparent: making conserves in past, or today for that matter, meant investing energy, time and money, and to see it all go bad because of a small distraction can give you a really bad heartache.

Giardiniera in Agrodolce
(Sweet and Sour Pickled Vegetables)

First, prepare the syrup, boiling water with salt and sugar for a few minutes. Turn off the heat, and as soon as it's cool, tip in the vinegar. Carefully clean the vegetables, remove the stalks, peel and so on, then dice or slice in similarly-sized pieces.

Sterilize the jars and lids, boiling them in water for at least 20 minutes. Fill them, squeezing the vegetables together up to the opening, so they'll shrink a bit. Fill with syrup and close the lid.

Place the sealed jars in a large pot filled to the brim with water, separating them with a few kitchen towels so that they don't crash into each other. Boil for 3 or 4 minutes while completely submerged, then turn off the heat and cool a bit before removing.

Store in a dry place without much light for 30 days before tasting.

INGREDIENTS

- 1 L WATER;
- 500 ML WHITE WINE VINEGAR;
- 250 GR SUGAR;
- 50 GR SALT;
- 250 GR CARROTS;
- 500 GR WHITE CAULIFLOWER;
- 300 GR GREEN BEANS;
- 250 GR CELERY ROOT;
- 150 GR CELERY;
- 250 GR ZUCCHINI;
- 250 GR SCALLIONS;
- 250 GR BELL PEPPERS;

Marmellata di Ciliegie *(Cherry Jam)*

INGREDIENTS

- 2 KG CHERRIES;
- 1,2 KG SUGAR;
- 1 LEMON ZEST;
- LEMON JUICE (1/2 LEMON'S WORTH);
- A PINCH OF SALT;
- 2 APPLES;
- A PINCH OF CINNAMON;
- 1 SACHET VANILLIN.

Wash the cherries and remove the stone, cut the apple in wedges without peeling and place everything in a large pot with sugar, lemon juice, lemon zest, a pinch of salt, cinnamon and vanillin, then vigorously stir together and let macerate for a few hours. Once ready, bring the mixture to boil, stir continuously and be careful that the water inside doesn't tip over. always check to see that the mixture doesn't stick to the bottom and stir once in a while.

After about an hour of cooking, check to see if the mixture is thick enough. My method is to drip some drops of mixture on a ceramic plate and see if it slides off quickly.

Take it out of the heat, filter in a narrow mesh strain or an electric mixer and then put it on the stove again for a few minutes, until it gains the right texture.

Store inside sterilized glass jars. Once you have filled and sealed the jars, continue sterilizing for at least 20 minutes, then take them out of the water and place them upside down on a flat surface, so that a vacuum forms when they cool.

Afterword

The adventure of writing a book is often motivated by the need to communicate with the outside world, conveying the character and personality of the writer. The composition, the topic, the wording, all evidently reveal different facets of the author's self.

Since I was only a boy I've nurtured a great curiosity towards food and cooking, diligently observing anyone who could teach me something. I was still young when I discovered the pains of preparing dishes and today I'm still deeply into it. Cooking is an activity that goes beyond the familiar four walls: it starts with a list of things to buy and ends with the chore of cleaning and putting back the tools of the trade.

I don't want my book to be an essay on cuisine that teaches you the exact steps for a perfect successful recipe, but a homely little handbook, to keep among the pots and pans, that helps us stay true to the traditions of cooking, with simple, healthy ingredients, prepared with the joy and care we reserve for our loved ones.

Index

A

B

C

D

F

G

I

L

M

N

P

Stampato da The Factory Srl - Roma
per conto di Borè Srl